MARKET FORECASTING

A Scientific Exposition on the Influence of Heavenly Bodies on Fluctuations of Values

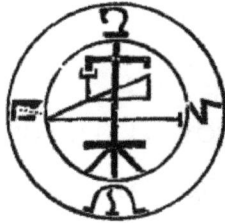

BY

Fakir Chandra Dutt

Cosmological Economics
www.CosmoEconomics.com

COSMOLOGICAL ECONOMICS

THE MASTERS OF FINANCIAL ASTROLOGY SERIES

The Masters of Financial Astrology Series brings together a collection of the most important classical and modern works on Astroeconomics or astrological financial market forecasting. These classic works written from the Golden Age of Technical Analysis to current times were carefully selected by the late Dr. Jerome Baumring of the Investment Centre Bookstore in the 1980's, as representing the most valuable and important works in financial astrology ever written. They were included as the foundational source texts for his program in advanced financial market analysis and forecasting, and serve as the ideal foundation for any analyst seeking a thorough education in astrological applications to financial market theory and forecasting.

The Golden Age of technical analysis was a period from the early 1900's through the 1960's where the foundational theories of modern financial analysis and financial astrology came into full form. The ideas and technologies developed during this fruitful period include the first serious research into the modern field of Astro-Economics, or Financial Astrology and related fields like cycle analysis, cosmic causation, solar influence on geomagnetic and Earthly events like weather, earthquakes, climate change and radio disturbance. Though financial astrology is actually a subject that stretches back centuries, if not millennia, this ripe period saw the real advent of popular research and theoretical development of this vast study of the interaction between cosmic forces and Earthly phenomena. This collection represents the best work available within this field.

Each quality reprint of these classical texts has been reproduced as an exact facsimile of the original text, maintaining the original layout, typeset, charts, and style of the author and time period, helping to preserve and communicate a sense of the feeling of the original work that a reproduction in modern format does not capture.

Many of these rare works and courses were originally printed in only very small private editions or as correspondence courses, so that the originals were easily lost or destroyed over time. Our reproductions of these important source works are printed on acid free paper and bound in a quality hardcover that will compliment any trading library and help to preserve this important resource for generations to come.

The series is also currently being digitized and archived for permanent digital preservation, creating a searchable reference library of market wisdom accessible globally and available in new digital formats to keep the knowledge fresh and accessible through new devices and technology as we advance further into the information revolution. To see our full catalog of hardcover reprints, new publications, and digital editions please visit our website at www.CosmoEconomics.com.

CONTENTS

নমো বিভিন্নজ্ঞেয়াংশ নমঃ স্মৃতিপথাতিগ।
নমস্ত্রিমূর্ত্তিভেদেন সর্গস্থিত্যন্তহেতবে ॥
বিশ্বায় বিশ্ববন্দ্যায় বিশ্বভূতাত্মনে নমঃ।
নমেহস্ত যোগিধ্যেয়ায় নমোহস্বধ্যাত্মরূপিণে ॥
দেবেশ কর্ম্ম সর্ব্বং মে ভবেদারাধনং তব ॥

Salutation to Thee
Who art beyond all remembrance ;
Obeisance to Thee
Oh Cause in threefold form
Of creation, maintenance and dissolution,
Knowable in Thy various partial appearances.
Salutation to Thee !
Thou art in the form of the whole Universe
And art worshipped by the whole Universe.
Thou art the self of all beings in the Universe ;
Salutation to Thee !
Thou art meditated upon by Yogins.
To Thee who art the Inner Self, obeisance.
All my actions should be worship of Thee.

PREFACE

The steller influence in human life and in all mundane affairs is now an undeniable fact. The astrological laws have stood the test of proof and any one who cares to study the subject with an open mind will find that he is dealing with immutable laws, not fanciful imaginings. We have now arrived at a stage where the science can speak for itself in the hands of any capable exponent. To the astrologer a door is open that is closed to other enquiries. He can take a glimpse behind the scenes and note the active power at work.

The chief aim of the present work is to show that the same laws of the planetary influence can be equally employed in forecasting the rise and fall in prices o. commodities, stocks and shares. No doubt, to foretell the market fluctuations, is a far more difficult task than the foretelling of events accomplished by the ancient astrologers. Nevertheless, it is possible by examining the records of the market prices in bygone years, and comparing them with the then relative positions of the planets, to formulate an empirical law by which we may predict that when certain celestial configurations shall recur certain effects on the Market will immediately follow. In this book an attempt has been made to find out the basic laws in this direction. I do not flatter myself that I have unearthed landmarks ; my only desire is to induce the reader personally to undertake researches for these. In the struggle to attain the truth the chief thing after all is not the finding, but the seeking. That man has done enough who can claim to have honestly searched.

The researches of the author were shared originally with small private groups as they were developed, and the techniques were subjected to continual test and refinement. The lessons then have been circulated privately among numerous students in various parts of the world since 1920, and it is most gratifying to find that many of the present day exponents of Market Forecasting follow these rules with very successful results. The present book represents a full and complete scientific exposition of the subject.

There are many of the topics discussed which I could have wished to consider more at length and illustrate them with many actual events from past records, but advancing years and declining health constrain me to husband my remaining energies in chiefly exposing the fundamental principles of Market Forecasting. Those who will follow these pages will learn that according to the astrological theory of Market Forecasting herein set forth, the planets indeed are potent in such affairs.

CALCUTTA :
1st May, 1949.

MARKET FORECASTING

INTRODUCTION

All motion in nature assumes a rhythmical character, a movement or swing to and fro, or up and down, or to right and left in alternate and continuous sequence and return ; a repeated succession of opposite states. However fluctuant be the occurrence of events, the course of commerce, of trade, of prosperity and adversity, of high and low prices exhibits a fairly regular order, and that this order tends to assume the recurrent and symmetric shape of a circle, so that the series of experiences, starting at any point on the circumference of the circle, proceeds successively through definite phases, as it travels, until it reaches the point of origin in the same place as that in which it began, when a corresponding career recommences, and so on *da capo*. But the cycle or circle of occurrences is not universally identical in its exact duration.

It would be a very useful thing if we were able to foretell when a rise or a fall was coming, but it is evidently impossible to predict such matters with certainty unless we find some corresponding ascertainable periodicity in nature.

If any steller body exerts an influence upon the earth, that influence must increase or decline as it approaches or recedes from us, and must vary in the whole course of its orbit ; hence it is reasonable to infer that certain phenomena in nature and in human life will recur at regular periods in accordance with the movements of heavenly bodies, just as day and night, summer and winter follow the course of the Sun. The extensive observations of the most ancient nations have conceived that the planets of the solar system have each a special influence upon man and upon the course of nature ; hence arose the most ancient and most wonderful of all sciences called Astrology. All kinds of events—wars, revolutions, new discoveries, fluctuations of commerce, bad or good harvests, may be foretold by a study of the planetary configurations, which can be easily ascertained beforehand for a long period in advance.

Astral science has beyond doubt established the truth that there is a strong connecting link between human events and planetary configurations, and that the rises and falls of the commercial and stock markets may be traced to certain planetary positions and aspects and are periodic. Wars, revolutions, political changes, new treaties of commerce, bad or good harvests, etc., may occur to decrease or increase the activity of trade. Nevertheless, it is wonderful how often a great commercial crisis has happened about

ten years after the previous one. It seems probable
that commercial crises are connected with a periodic
variation of weather, affecting all parts of the earth,
and probably arising from increased waves of heat
received from the Sun at average intervals of about
ten years. A greater supply of heat increases the
harvests, and a falling off in the Sun's heat makes bad
harvests. These times are regulated by organic law.
Germination is the effect of the combined influences
of the Sun and Moon, and unless that time be selected
for sowing when these combined influences are in
force, failure is sure to be the result. These combined
influences are in greatest force for from two days before
the last quarter of the Moon, until two days after the
new moon.

Prof. Jevons pointed out the connection between
sun-spots and corresponding events on the earth, for
he perceived that the periods of occurrence of the
maximum sun-spots coincided with fruitful harvests
and periods during which spots may be totally absent
from the Sun's disc coincided with poor harvests and
commercial derangement. The period of this cycle
lasts about 10-11 years. He considered that the first
three years of this cycle generally witness depressed
trade, with want of employment, falling prices, and
much poverty ; then there will be perhaps three years
of active, healthy trade, with moderately rising prices
and improving credit, then followed by two years of
excited trade. In the ninth year a bubble rapidly
forms which, in the tenth year is pricked and ends in

a collapse. It is not to be supposed that things go as regularly as is here stated ; sometimes the cycle lasts only nine, or even eight years, instead of ten ; minor bubbles and crises sometimes happen in the course of the cycle, and disturb its regularity. If the sun-spots cycle trade fluctuations could be finally established it would tell very greatly in favour of planetary influences ; for although the sun-spot periodicity may occasionally synchronize with epochs of rise and fall in prices, yet it must not be forgotten that both phenomena depend upon planetary influence. The systematic observations upon the sun-spots have served conclusively to establish that these have their immediate origin in some action of the planets Jupiter, Saturn, Venus and others upon the photosphere of the Sun, and other planetary influences like the perihelion and aphelion of Jupiter, which generally correspond in a very remarkable manner with periods of low death-rate.

Certain commodities have besides their seasonal variation in price, also particular periods of rise and fall in price. Cotton, for example, has a period of 10 and 11 years. Iron follows a periodicity of about the same years. But there are effects of particular planetary influence, which upset to a greater or lesser extent the plain sailing of these cycles.

Also it has been observed that the rise and fall of prices in the Market always occur in cycles of 19 years. This cycle has a relation to the movement of the Moon's North Node in the signs of the zodiac.

The movement of the Node is always against the order of the signs and when it passes through the sign Leo, we have an excited trade and the prices reach to a very high point. As the Node passes through the signs Cancer and Gemini the prices though above normal are on the decline, and when it reaches Taurus the prices become normal. After that with the passage of the Node through Aries and Pisces, the prices gradually fall below normal and when it reaches the sign Aquarius the prices come to the lowest level. Next with the passage of the Node through the signs Capricorn and Sagittarius the prices gradually tend to rise and come to normal as soon as it reaches the sign Scorpio. After this the prices again tend to rise gradually above normal as the Node passes through the signs Libra and Virgo, and come to the highest level when it reaches the sign Leo again.

Although this cycle of 19 years may be considered as the general trend of the price curve, it does not follow in strict regularity. There are other secondary factors found within the cycle, which distort the curve and in consequence a low business trend may be changed to a higher one and a higher trend may become lowered. Nevertheless, it is wonderful how the cycle follows the course of ups and downs according to the passage of the Node through the zodiacal signs in spite of war or peace or other interfering causes. The scondary factors which affect the plain sailing of the cycle are the conjunction and aspects between the major superior planets. Hence unless the planetary

influence be taken into account, no real cycle of
Market fluctuations can be determined, and no forecast
of the general trend of prices for any particular period
can be correctly made.

Variations of the weather and fluctuations of values
in the Market have been observed to coincide with
the conjunction, opposition and parallel of declination
(particularly of the same denomination) of the planets ;
and also, with the difference of longitudes, called the
major "aspects" of 60, 90 and 120 degrees between
those bodies. When minor "aspects" or differences
of longitude of 30, 36, 45, 72, 135, 144 and 150 degrees
are formed between the planets slight weather variations and market fluctuations are found to coincide,
but they are not so important nor so lasting as
those which coincide with the major aspects before
mentioned. The crossing of the equator and the tropics
by the larger planets, and their perihelion, also are
found by observation to produce atmospheric disturbances as well as fluctuations in the price of commodities.

Prices are inclined to follow a "pendulum" movement, rising and falling gradually, although not necessarily regularly. It may be that a swing of the pendulum may be lasting longer than another, but this
does not alter the fact that the movements are
periodic. One can therefore ascertain when a stock
will increase in value or its price fall, month by month,
or during a certain period, from the planetary configurations. But the degree of rise or fall, that is, the

exact points by which it will rise or fall cannot be definitely estimated, although the advantage of rise and fall in the two periods may be obtained.

Commercial and financial crises are the results of many causes, and invariably follow abnormal declines in prices ; they are the effects of causes which are beyond the control of the human mind and are confined to no creed, party or politics. In a crisis, the ruinous fall in prices manifests itself in stocks and shares more than in commodities. Every serious political disturbance or revolution is likely to be attended by a crisis. Neither law nor legislative enactments, tariff or any great monopoly can stem the tide of planetary cycles causing the crisis. When the periods or cycles arrive for a crisis, the market prices take a downward tendency until the crisis has ended, when a newer or greater demand begins to open up and ascending prices prevail according to the phases of the planetary cycles.

CHAPTER I

Planetary Influences

The ancients consulted the stars for the purpose of reading in their movements the vicissitudes of human affairs. Astrologers cast their horoscopes, and showed how the career of man was predicted in the configurations of the planets at his birth. Statesmen sought the stars for guidance in the affairs of the empire; while a decision on all matters of moment could only be safely taken after consultation with the heavens. Hence there is no reason why the same principles should not be applied in consideration of the fluctuation of prices of stocks, shares and commodities.

Knowing the important parts played by the aspects between the major planets and taking into consideration also the fact that certain aspects between the planets have a strong influence on human affairs and also on the physical world itself, it will soon be clear that we must first turn our attention to these.

It has been observed that the movements of the market generally are indicated by the general major aspects formed between the larger planets. They indicate the tendencies for long periods. The larger or major planets are Pluto, Neptune, Uranus, Saturn and Jupiter. The influence of Pluto has not yet been fully understood. Generally the good and evil aspects between the planets foreshadow the rise and fall of general business conditions and market prices.

The aspects between the planets are certain definite distances in longitude between them. They are classified as good and evil. The good aspects are of 30, 60, 120 and 150 degrees in distance ; the aspects formed by distances of 36, 72 and 144 degrees are slightly good ; and the evil aspects are of 45, 90, 135 and 180 degrees. The conjunction is good or evil according to the nature of the planets. The conjunction between Jupiter and Uranus is considered good, while that between Saturn and Uranus, evil. The conjunction between Jupiter and Saturn is generally considered as good but somewhat of a doubtful nature and it often shows a rise. The good aspects indicate rise and the evil, fall.

The conjunction and aspects work within certain orbs. Their influences commence when they just come at the beginning of the orb and attain the maximum when they are exact and then come to an end when they are out of the orb. The orb of influence for a conjunction or a major aspect is generally about 6 to 8 degrees, 3 to 4 degrees before reaching and the same number of degrees after seperating from the exact place of the conjunction or the aspect. In the case of minor aspects and parallel of declination, an orb of 1 degree is allowed. The influence of parallel of declination depends on the aspect between the two planets formed about their parallel position, and when a good aspect is formed the result is good, and with an evil aspect, the result is evil. The parallel enhances the effect of the aspect. Generally it may be considered as a conjunction.

The aspects of major planets show the principal business trend. When there are two or more aspects of a similar nature operating at the same time, and no contrary aspects found, the indications are nearly certain of fulfilment. But when the aspects are of contrary nature, the effects are more or less uncertain, and will lean to one side or the other according to the preponderance or strength of a particular kind of aspects. At various times the aspects are formed with planets either retrograde or stationary, at these times generally the effects are more potent.

Whenever there is a maximum of conjunctions or oppositions of two or more of the superior planets crises in market prices either coincide or immediately follow. The planet Jupiter joins or opposes Saturn every ten years, and we find that trade crisis has synchronized with either the conjunction or opposition of these two great planets. The conjunction or opposition of Uranus occurs every seven years, and this is a number constantly recurring in the periodicity of great crises. The conjunction or opposition of Jupiter and Neptune comes very nearer to this, occurring a little more than every six years. The conjunction or opposition of Saturn and Neptune recurs about every 17 or 18 years, and this configuration has frequently synchronized with such crises. The conjunction of Mars and Jupiter occurs in every two years and generally indicates a crisis.

For each year the aspects between the major planets are to be calculated. These are between Uranus and Neptune, Saturn and Neptune, Jupiter and Neptune, Saturn and Uranus, Jupiter and Uranus and Jupiter and Saturn. The position and aspects of the Moon's North Node are to be noted as they are also important.

The aspects between Neptune and other major planets show a too long cycle for any practical usefulness and show no outstanding effects and are not therefore dependable indicators.

The conjunction and harmonious aspects of Jupiter to Saturn or Uranus, and its conjunction with the Moon's North Node, and also the favourable aspects of Saturn to Uranus establish a long trend of advancing stock prices and business activity ; the conjunction and evil aspects of Saturn to Uranus, and to the Node show depression and declining prices. The evil aspects of Jupiter are not very significant, but still show a little downward tendency. Harmonious and inharmonious aspects to Pluto are also considered by some to have effects according to the nature of the aspects. As these planets break away from adverse positions or aspects and advance towards harmony, depression gives way to more confidence and gradually as they get nearer to the favourable aspect positions, the clouds of business break up and another cycle of prosperity commences.

At various times a retrograde movement, stationary position and again direct movement of the planets are observed. If these happen to be in close aspect to another planet at the same time, the effects are most potent. When Uranus, Neptune or Pluto changes its degree of longitude or its direction of movement (direct or retrograde) frequently a change in the prevailing trend in political or economical condition takes place, as the movement of these planets is very slow and they retain their positions for a long time.

The number of favourable aspects greater in a year indicates a good and prosperous year, and the greater the number of evil aspects, the more depressing results may expected. The rise in prices depends on the presence of favourable and absence of unfavourable aspects. The fall depends on the presence of more unfavourable and absence of favourable aspects. When the aspects are strongest, if harmonious, the top is registered, if inharmonious, the bottom.

A *boom* indicates a state of numerous transactions with an appreciably augmented price. It is caused by the successive good aspects or benefic conjuctions of various planets without any interposing evil aspects to break the series.

A *slump* signifies a sudden heavy fall in prices and is due to a succession of evil aspects between the planets without any intervening good aspects to break the series.

Prices *harden* when they tend to advance upward ; they are *easier*, when a somewhat lower quotation can be obtained than existed before.

Neptune is very slow in action, depressive in nature and with a tendency to lower prices.

Uranus signifies increase in value and a sudden fluctuation in prices, particularly when strongly and favourably aspected ; otherwise the contrary is shown with evil aspects.

Saturn exercises a depressing influence, causing downward changes in market values. As it is slow in action, its favourable strong aspects tend to steady prices, which slowly advance.

Jupiter is always good and expanding, favouring higher prices and its strong benefic aspects generally bring a rise in the stock market, no matter what the article may be.

In financial matters and market produce favourable aspects of Mars indicate sudden rise in prices, but its evil aspects have a depressive influence, bringing sudden downfalls in prices. A strong aspect with Saturn or Neptune generally brings strange and sudden changes and much excitement according to the nature of the aspect. Mars favourably aspecting Uranus, points to higher prices, but probablity of scares and excitement. But its influence does not last long.

To trace a connection between the rise and fall periods of a trade cycle, it would be advisable to examine those planetary aspects and the position of the Moon's North Node in the signs of the zodiac which cover about the same interval of time. A comparison can best be made by means of "graph" curves. If we take into consideration the mean value of the prices for each entire year, we shall find a curve which has a connection with the economic indication for a period of some years together.

In the diagram below the yearly curve of the Index Numbers of Wholesale Prices in Calcutta of commodities is shown for the years 1933 to 1942 and also the positions of the Node and the aspects of the major planets prevalent during each year are shown at the bottom.

The merest glance at the figure shows that the

Node is moving from Pisces in 1932 to Aquarius in 1933-34, when the price level was the lowest. From this period the price began gradually to rise, supported by the good aspects and rose to the highest level in 1943 when the Node reached Leo. It appears that the minor evil aspects of Jupiter did not affect the natural tendency and with the benefic aspects in 1943, the price level came to more than 200 points above normal. The fluctuations due to the influence of the good and evil strong aspects of the major planets are clearly discernable and from 1939 the sextile aspect of Uranus and Jupiter and also from 1940 the conjunction of Jupiter and Saturn and also that of Saturn and Uranus marked the crisis.

The conjunctions and oppositions of the major planets in almost every case coincide with commercial crises. Observing the aspects between Saturn and Uranus, we find that their influence is considerably longer, and their effects can consequently last over a protracted period. In the above case the conjunctions of Jupiter with Saturn and Uranus influenced for several years after 1942 and brought the great famine period in India, particularly in Bengal, when the prices of all commodities rose to the highest level never witnessed before.

No man in his senses ever averred or implied that these planetary influences were the causes of trade crises, but no one can read history without remarking how often these phenomena coincided with such crises. History shows that the joint conjunction or opposition of Jupiter, Saturn, Uranus and Neptune never yet occurred without some great crisis coinciding or immediately following.

FOUNDATION OF CALCUTTA

CHAPTER II

Planetary Configurations

As has already been stated that the influence of the configurations of the major planets lasts for a longer period, but there occur short intermediate configurations with the smaller planets, which either bring a sharp accelaration of the existing long trend or a temporary reversal in the opposite direction according to the nature of the configurations.

The minor planets Mars, Venus and Mercury form aspects with the major planets and with each other in rapid sequence, and except when these planets are retrograde or stationary, their aspects do not remain in force for a long time, and consequently their effects on the market are brief.

The conjunctions, oppositions and other aspects of Mars, Venus and Mercury are formed with intervals of some months or days. These configurations seem to show a definite influence according to the same laws which we have found for those between the larger planets. But the much smaller duration of these periods seems to coincide with the continual fluctuations of prices going on day by day, and shown in

2

the monthly reports of the financial newspapers. Moreover these fluctuations are practically universal and are valid for a large number of different articles.

Of the smaller planets, the influence of the configurations of Mars with the major planets has moderately longer duration and consequently its effects are more lasting than those of Venus and Mercury. But when all these smaller planets are retrograde or stationary they have decided effects as intermediate indicators, otherwise their influences, particularly those of Venus and Mercury are not very remarkable. Also when the configurations of these minor planets are similar or confirmatory to the nature of those between the major planets, the effects should be more pronounced and when their nature is contrary, their influence cannot be expected to have much effect.

Nevertheless it is not surprising that the coincidence may not be here so striking as in the case for the longer periodic influences. For, it must be noted that this smaller trend is subservient to the longer trend and cannot materially change the general indications.

In the case of solar and lunar configurations they transmit the influence of the aspects of other planets. Suppose there is an evil aspect between Mars and Jupiter, and the Sun comes in conjunction with Mars, the effects take place eariler, as hastened by the quick moving Sun.

As it is generally supposed that all good aspects will tend to produce a rising market, and adverse aspects, a falling market, so it will be well to note all such aspects in sequence and forecasts may be made accordingly. But this will not be found always correct, for adverse aspects to Jupiter and good aspects to Saturn have to be carefully considered.

Each kind of stocks or commodities has its individual ruling planet, as will be found in the chapter on significators, but as a rule, most of the stocks move in a similar curve.

It has already been said that the movements of the market is indicated by the aspects formed between the major planets. They indicate the tendencies for longer periods; the minor planets cause the smaller day-to-day fluctuations.

Planets are strong in their own signs or in their signs of exaltation, and are weak in the signs of their detrement or fall, or when retrograde. A planet coming to an aspect of a retrograde planet gets no good effect from a good aspect, but if it forms an evil aspect, the evil effect is enhanced. But when it has also a good aspect from another planet at the same time, the good aspect of the retrograde planet will bring good effects.

The Sun rules the Government Stocks and Securities. Generally all markets are affected more or less, by the strength of such securities. When consols are low, the market tends to sag and fall, rarely rising very high; when consols are high, the market has a rising tendency. Hence the Sun may be considered as an important factor in the rise and fall of markets, also the Moon has a secondary influence.

The aspects of Mercury and the Sun are strong on the stock market, the conjunction and parallel of declination, however, may bring some panic in the market. The parallel of declination of Mercury with Jupiter and the Sun at the same time, makes a very steady market.

The Sun's aspects are slightly good or bad according to their nature, but much will depend on the aspects between the other planets to which he applies. For example, if the Sun comes to a good aspect of Uranus, he favours slight advance, and an evil aspect, a similar effect downward, but if Uranus has a good aspect to another planet, and if the aspect is a close one, the good aspect of the Sun will bring a good advance in the market ; but if the aspect of Uranus is evil, an evil aspect of the Sun will bring a marked fall. The Sun square or opposition or in parallel declination to Jupiter and Uranus makes a very active market, though sometimes very weak, when the aspect begins to form and very strong, when it separates or *vice versa*.

The lunar aspects depend upon the aspects of the Sun. If the Sun has a close good aspect, the good aspects of the Moon, when close, will be rather strong for advance, and an evil aspect of the Moon to an evil planet is only slightly weak ; but if the Sun be in a close evil aspect to Saturn or Uranus, the good aspects of the Moon have little strength and evil aspects may be quite strong to cause breaks. Mars well aspected by the Moon or Mercury advances the market, but the evil aspects bring slight fall.

Also the movements or changes in the market are generally shown in a minor way in conformity with the prevailing aspects between the major planets in the quarterly changes of the phases of the Moon, and the latitude in which it is found at the time. The Moon in North latitude will indicate an upward tendency ; in South latitude, its influence indicates downward inclination. When the Moon changes at its quarters from the South to the North latitude, it points to an upward tendency in prices ; when it changes towards the South latitude, fluctuations are somewhat uncertain and rapid, with lowering prices. The strongest and most favourable influences will be experienced when the Moon is quartering between Cancer and Libra or when it is passing from Pisces to Gemini, though the latter is not so strong. The other quarterings are usually weak. The change of Moon is generally indicative of the direction the markets are likely to take for the coming week. It has been found that when the Moon enters Aries each month, the markets have invariably advanced, sometimes slightly, other times considerably ; in many cases, stocks have held firmly when the Moon entered the sign and the influences lasted several days before waning. If in addition to the entry of the Moon in Aries, Mercury and Venus happen to be strong in northern signs, the advance would be more certain and lasting.

The effects of the solar and lunar configurations are exceedingly shorter in duration and very often last for a short time, sometimes for an hour or so. It is therefore not necessary to consider them always, except in the case of eclipses.

The influence of the Moon is somewhat modified for rises and falls by the aspects and latitude of Mercury. Mercury, like the Moon, in a north latitude favours an upward tendency; therefore when the Moon and Mercury are both north, stronger rises may be expected; while, on the other hand, when Mercury and the Moon are in a south latitude, lowering prices may be anticipated. Should Mercury, however, be north, and the Moon south, or *vice versa*, conflicting market prices will result. But Mercury alone is very unimportant; when aspected by the Sun with the Moon and Mercury in the south latitude, though their influences are small, the market will be very unreliable. When Mars is in a strong aspect with Mercury, strange and sudden changes and much excitement may be looked for. A favourable aspect of Mars points to higher prices, but with probability of scares and excitement, and with the Moon north and Mercury south latitude, or *vice versa*, the influence of Mars will point to either rapid rises or sudden and unexpected falls. When Jupiter is favourably aspected by Mercury, with the Moon and Mercury both north, very rapid upward tendendy may be expected, and it will be all the more rapid should the Sun also be in good aspect to Jupiter. Jupiter's influence, whenever Mercury, Moon and Mars are in south latitude, should be very judiciously considered, for his strong aspects will avert a slump or downfall ; in fact, the evil aspects of the other planets will always be modified by the good aspects of Jupiter.

When there are aspects between two or three of the major planets and Mercury forms a conjunction, sextile or trine aspect with any of them, when within an orb of one or two degrees of the aspect, it will cause a brisk market. Similarly, if two or three major planets are in evil aspects and Mercury also forms an exact conjunction, parallel, square or opposition aspect with any of them at the same time, a quick break or fall will follow. Saturn is generally slow in action, and when strongly aspected by Mars with the Moon and Mercury in north latitude, scares and rapidly increased values may be looked for. Saturn and Mercury in north latitude generally tend to steady prices.

Venus exercises but little influence on the financial market, except on the cotton, sugar, jute markets, perfumes and ladies' proprietary articles, and fancy goods. But still the conjunction and good aspects of Venus with Jupiter and Uranus show a rise, but have not much effect with Saturn. The evil aspects with Jupiter have not much noticeable effect, while with Saturn, show depressing results.

All the above indications are always to be considered as secondary, and by themselves will not always indicate any definite results unless supported by the the indications from the aspects between the major planets.

The conjunction and evil aspects of Mars with Saturn, Uranus or Neptune indicate fall, while with Jupiter show much fluctuation, either a rise or a fall. Similarly with the aspects of the major planets among themselves. The good aspects favour a rise, while evil aspects, a fall.

The general trend of the stock and share market may therefore be ascertained from the ephemeral aspects of the planets as described above.

As an example, let us consider the trend and the fluctuations of the market from the planetary aspects for the month of June, 1946. The aspects are noted for each date and the values of a few different kinds of shares in Calcutta Market for certain specific dates are given.

1946 June Date	Aspects Major Planets	Minor Planets	Other Notes	Govt. Paper Rs. As.
1		Merc. par. Uranus	Merc. N. Lat. 1 to 30	
3	Mars semi-sq. Uranus		Moon N. Lat. 1 to 14	
4		Merc. trine Jupiter, conj. Uranus	Moon S. Lat. 15 to 27	103 1

1946 June Date	Aspects Major Planets	Minor Planets	Other Notes	Govt. Paper Rs. As.
6		Merc. sextile Mars	MoonN.Lt. 28 to 30	103 .10
7		Venus sq. Jupiter		
8		Sun trine Jupiter		
9		Sun conj. Uranus		103 8
12	Jupiter trine Uranus	Venus conj. Saturn		
13		Merc. sq. Neptune		
14		Mercury par. Uranus	Lunar Eclipse	
16		Merc. semi- sq. Mars		104 6
19		Merc. sq. Jupiter		
20		Venus semi- sq. Uranus		
22			Moon enters Aries	
23		Venus sextile Neptune		
24	Mars semi- sq. Jupiter	Sun sextile Mars		

1946 June Date	Aspects Major Planets	Minor Planets	Other Notes	Govt. Paper Rs. As.
24		Merc. conj. Saturn		104 10
28		Merc. par. Saturn		104 15
30		Merc. semi-sq. Uranus		103 0

1946 June Date	Jute (Howrah) Rs. As.	Textile (New Victoria) Rs. As.	Engn. (Indian Iron) Rs. As.	Sugar (Belsund) Rs. As.	Tea (Biswa-nath) Rs. As.
4	136 12	8 9	57 0	15 5	
6	135 0	8 10	57 12		54 8
9	136 8	8 8	59 0	15 8	55 12
16	138 0	8 8	61 4		
24	146 0	8 9	63 0	16 1	61 4
26	147 3	9 6	64 8	16 3	61 8
30	145 0	10 0	64 0	17 2	63 8
July 31	163 0	12 4	64 0	20 2	
Aug 11	171 0	13 4			65 8
Sept 17	145 0	10 0	55 12	15 8	
24	145 12	10 11	54 13	14 8	59 0

From the above tables it will be evident from the trine aspect between the major planets Jupiter and Uranus, that the general trend will be a general rise in the market and this will continue for some time until a strong adverse aspect between two major planets occurs, (the semi-square aspect of Mars with Uranus and Jupiter is weak). From the Ephemeris it will be found that again on the 30th July following there was a trine aspect between the same planets. On the 11th August next, Mars was in sextile aspect with Saturn and on the 12th September, Mars was in trine to Uranus, followed by Mars conjunction Jupiter on the 24th September. This showed a boom in the market and the aspect of Mars with Uranus brought some unexpected changes about the 12th September, and the conjunction of Mars with Jupiter brought a crisis and sudden collapse of the market ! The different kinds of aspects between the minor planets in June clearly show the petty temporary fluctuations in prices and require no comments.

It should, however, be noted that when there is an aspect between the planets on a certain date and no other aspect occurs for the space of five days or more, then a transition point is formed, which is always midway between the dates. Thus, in the above instance, the trine aspect between Mars and Uranus happened on the 12th September and the conjunction of Mars with Jupiter occurred on the 24th September, the transition date therefore falls on the 17th September. The trend of the market actually changed towards the crisis from about this date.   When the transition point occurs between aspects of the same nature, that is, both good or both bad, then it will denote that of the greatest intensity, that is, the highest rise or the lowest fall, according to the nature of the aspects.

Market trends are the results of many forces and do not depend solely on one kind of influence. Though the configurations of the major planets indicate the general tendency of the market and the confirmatory aspects of the minor planets regulate the fluctuations, yet all these alone do not always indicate the variations of values in the individual markets, such as, Bombay, Calcutta, London, New York, etc., correctly. There are other factors to be considered, such as planetary configurations, transits, etc., found in the horoscopes for the local Stock Exchanges and also in horoscopes of concerns in the country in question, and these are explained in the following chapters.

CHAPTER III

Mundane Astrology

A résumé of Mundane Astrology will be of great value to the students and a brief outline is therefore given here, particularly with regard to weather, crop and market conditions.

Ingress :

The exact moment of the ingress of the Sun into Aries, the commencement of the Vernal Equinox, is the commencement of the astrological year. A Map of the Heavens is drawn for this moment of ingress at the seat of the Government. Similar figures are to be cast for the Sun's ingresses into Cancer, Libra and Capricorn for determining the principal events during the ensuing quarters of the year. It is stated that when a fixed sign ascends in the Vernal Equinox figure, the horoscope will rule the whole year ; but if a common sign ascends, it will rule for six months ; and when a cardinal sign ascends, the figure will rule for three months. But it must be noted that the Vernal Equinox figure always rules the ensuing year and the other ingress figures are subsidiary to it.

The First House of a Mundane Horoscope indicates the country and its people, and their condition of prosperity and health.

The Second House shows the wealth of the nation, revenue, taxation, banks, stock exchange, trade.

The Third House indicates all means of inland transit, railways, road and river traffic, motor service ; post office, telegraphs and telephones ; newspapers, magazines, ephemeral publications ; neighbouring nations.

The Fourth House shows lands, crops, produce of the land, mines, buildings ; owners of land and workers on it ; opposition party in the Government.

The Fifth House indicates places of amusement, entertainment and pleasure ; theatres, cinemas, sports, etc. ; schools, children, birth-rate.

The Sixth House indicates public health and sickness ; national services : army, navy, civil service ; workers and employees.

The Seventh House shows foreign affairs, war, public foes, foreign trade, marriages, divorce.

The Eighth House indicates public mortality, death duties, etc.

The Ninth House shows shipping, long distance traffic, cables, wireless telegraphy, religion, law courts, judges, universities, professors, scientific institutions and publications.

The Tenth House indicates the monarch, president, the Government, persons in authority, royalty, eminent and famous persons.

The Eleventh House represents Parliament, Councils, Municipal bodies, ministers, friends of the nation ; legislation.

The Twelfth House represents prisons, workhouses, hospitals, asylums, criminals, secret foes, etc.

The strongest parts of a mundane horoscope are the first, tenth, seventh and the fourth houses ; next, the eleventh, ninth, eighth and twelfth ; and afterwards the remaining houses below the horizon.

Planets ascending and the Moon, unless Cancer is found in the tenth, are the significators of the people ; and the planets culminating represent the Government.

The planet ascending or the Moon in benefic aspect with Venus or Jupiter and more than 17 degrees distant from the Sun—people will be prosperous, healthy and safe in their possessions during the rule of the Ingress.

Any planet ascending or the Moon be within 17 degrees of the Sun and afflicted by the malefics—people will be unfortunate, sickly and insecure in their possessions.

An evil planet ascending will show an unhealthy season and some misfortune, riots, loss of property and life will fall on the people.

A benefic planet ascending and not afflicted by a malefic and has the application of the Moon by conjunction or a benefic aspect, will show that the people will be prosperous, successful and secure.

Any planet ascending or the Moon afflicted by a

malefic from the 8th house, shows great mortality during the ensuing quarter.

A planet in an angle house, or particularly close to the cusp of the 4th house and also in evil aspects, influences the weather according to its nature. Saturn has been observed to increase cold and moisture; Jupiter and Mars are of a caloric character; Neptune and Venus, temperate and moist; Uranus, cold and moist; Mercury, variable and windy. A malefic in the 4th house generally afflicts the Government through its opposition to the 10th house.

If the ascending planet or the Moon is afflicted by Mars from the 7th house, danger of war, riot are shown. People will be much annoyed by their enemies. But if the affliction comes from the 4th house by Saturn and Mars in the sign Taurus, Gemini, Leo or Scorpio, there will be great danger of earthquakes, of deaths by accidents in mines and falls of houses and buildings.

When the ruler of the ascending sign is afflicted, the people will generally suffer.

When Mars is afflicted and Aries rising—misfortune by heat or drought, brain fever, etc. Scorpio rising—misfortune by flood, venomous creatures, etc.

When Venus is afflicted and Taurus rising—extremity of cold; fruits destroyed. Libra rising—storms, pestilence.

When Mercury is afflicted and Gemini rising—corrupt air, storms; lungs and bronchial troubles. Virgo rising—cold and dryness, scarcity of the products of the earth; intestinal troubles.

When Cancer rises and the Moon is afflicted—damage by excessive rain ; head and stomach troubles.

When Leo rises and the Sun is afflicted—damage through heat and drought ; pestilence ; diseases of the heart and nerves.

When Jupiter is afflicted and Sagittarius rises—fevers and infirmities. Pisces rises—inundations ; infirmities of feet, gout, dropsy.

When Saturn is afflicted and Capricorn rises—extreme cold and dry weather ; misfortune and disease. Aquarius rising—moist air, high winds.

From the Ingress Map of the Vernal Equinox the Ruler of the year is to be determined. For the Ruler of the year take the planet ascending, or in the tenth house, or receiving the application aspect of any of the luminaries from any other angle. When there is no planet in the ascendant or in the tenth house, the planet posited in the 7th or 4th is to be taken. When there is no planet in an angle, only the planet configurated with the luminaries is to be taken.

When the Ruler of the year is in benefic aspect with the ruler of the sign in which it is posited and free from afflictions, the people will be in good condition, secure and at peace. When it is afflicted and in no configuration with its dispositor, the people will be fearful, troubled with war, anxiety, strikes, etc. According to the house in which the Ruler is located, will the good or evil condition of the people be shown.

Sun, free from affliction—the monarch and nobles

3

will be in good condition. Corn and cattle will be plentiful ; people prosperous.

Sun afflicted—nobles suffer diminution of power and privileges.

Moon well aspected—people healthy and fortunate. If afflicted—the contrary.

Mercury well aspected—scientific men, artists, students, school teachers, merchants will have a successful year. If afflicted—the contrary.

Venus well aspected—women will be advantaged ; people thrive and be much given to sport and mirth. If afflicted—women will be unfortunate, cases of cruelty will be numerous ; people unfortunate.

Mars well aspected—soldiers fortunate and victorious ; people prosperous. If afflicted—the contrary.

Jupiter well aspected—measures of reform ; prosperity ; people contented. If afflicted—little benefit ; misfortune.

Saturn well aspected—great impetus to building ; the earth will be fruitful. If afflicted—cold weather ; losses, damage by winds, storms, rain ; much mortality among the aged.

Uranus well aspected—benefit to town councils, public bodies, societies, incorporated bodies ; new inventions ; gain in railways, electricity, aviation. If afflicted—strikes, rioting, rebellion, explosions.

Neptune well aspected—extension of democratic power ; benefits in matters of art, etc. If afflicted—collapse, downfall, chaotic condition of affairs, scandals, various forms of crime and vice ; political instability.

Consider the house in which the Ingress falls. All matters governed by that house will come to the fore during the period ruled over by the Ingress, and the effects will be good or evil according to the aspects and the house and position of the aspecting planet.

When the Sun's Ingress into Aries rules for a longer period, all other solar Ingresses occurring within that period will have a secondary influence to such Ingress into Aries. In the Ingress figure deal with the houses from the first house in rotation. Note particularly the planets therein and the aspects they receive, and where there is no planet in a house, consider the ruler of the house and its aspects and judge according thereto.

The particular day or dates of various events indicated in the Ingress figure can be obtained from the transits of the Sun and the planets over the places and the aspect positions of the planets in the Ingress figure. Also by directions the dates of the events can be ascertained, which will be explained later on.

In order to ascertain the character of the weather and crop conditions during a particular season, for a particular locality, the date and time of the entry of the Sun in the four cardinal signs of the zodiac, Aries, Cancer, Libra and Capricorn, for the place where a particular production is abundant, must be ascertained from the Ephemeris for the year, and a horoscope is erected for the concerned place. From these horoscopes the weather and crop conditions for any particular season is to be judged in the following manner :

1. Planets in the fourth house are to be considered with their aspects.

2. When there is no planet in the fourth house, the planet in the tenth house and its aspects are to be considered.

3. If there are no planets in either of the fourth or the tenth houses, the planets in other angle houses (ascendant and descendant) of the horoscope with their aspects are to be considered.

4. When there are no planets in any of the angular houses of the horoscope, the ruler of the fourth house with its aspects is to be examined and considered.

We generally find that drought occurs under the combined influences of Mars and Jupiter, just as great damage to the crops occurs under the combined influences of Saturn and Uranus ; and Jupiter or Venus gives very favourable crop condition, but the greatest rainfall damaging the crops is under the combined influences of Venus and Saturn, when these planets are in one of the angle houses of the Ingress horoscope, particularly when in aspect with the Sun.

If at the autumnal equinox the planets Uranus and Saturn be in angles and in aspect with the Sun, the autumnal crops will suffer ; if at the following winter solstice the same planets be again in angular houses, the winter will be severe and crops will suffer or there will be great rise in prices ; and if at the vernal ingress they are similarly placed, the spring crops will fail or be late. On the other hand, if Jupiter be in one of the angular houses, the crop conditions will be fine. But if both Mars and Jupiter are so situated, drought will follow. If Venus be so situated, much rain will follow and good crop prospects are indicated.

If at the vernal equinox the Sun and Saturn are in conjunction in one of the angle houses, the season will be disastrous to agriculturists and the crop condition will suffer. When they are in aspects, particularly in the winter solstice, some damage to the crops are to be feared. If at the vernal equinox Saturn is near the lower meridian and Jupiter and Mercury are in the ascendant, or Uranus is in conjunction with the Sun and Jupiter in the seventh house and is in square aspect with Mars in the fourth house, the spring is very backward and the harvest is deficient and very late. When in the summer solstice Uranus is in the ascendant and Mercury near the lower meridian, similar results are shown. When at the summer solstice Mars is in conjunction with Saturn in the fourth house and Jupiter is in the ascendant, the summer crops will not be very bad, but some retardation of growth may be feared.

The influence of Neptune will be similar to Venus.

New Moons :

New Moons or Neomena or Lunations are next in significance to the four Ingresses. Such maps have a decided significance in most cases in connection with current events, when the place of the conjunction of the two luminaries falls in close strong aspect with some planet or very near an angle of the nearest Ingress horoscope, otherwise they will not be of much importance. The New Moons following within the period of an Ingress, in addition to being referred to the previous Ingress, should also be referred to the figure of the Sun's Ingress into Aries.

Generally the Lunations will bring the matter connected with the house of the Ingress in which they will fall, to the front, good or evil according to the aspects received. They also influence the weather when there is any planet in the angles of the Lunation map.

Saturn—high wind, dark clouds ; in hot weather, lessening of heat ; in winter, cold augmented.

Mars—heat is increased in summer ; cold in winter diminished ; spring or autumn, inclines to heat rather than cold.

Jupiter, Venus, Moon—a temperate, good and wholesome weather ; fruits of the earth increase, good cultivation.

Mercury, Uranus—storms and high winds.

Transits and Conjunctions.

Transits and conjunctions of the major planets in a sign exert a strong influence upon countries ruled by it. Also they may be regarded as changes taking place within the map of the current solar Ingress and producing results according to the nature of the house in which they fall.

Transits :

> Neptune—Great changes of a democratic nature ; increasing power of the people and popular movements. If afflicted, weakening of the ruling power.

> Uranus—Important reforms and changes in the Government. National desires may be awakened and may find expression in reforms or aggressive measures. If afflicted, strikes, riots, wars, revolution, panics ; the Government suffers ; market effects are disturbing and inflationary.

> Saturn—Hindrance and misfortune ; epidemics. Bad for the Government. Failure of legislative measures. Commercial depression.

> Jupiter—Prosperity, increase of trade ; good health of people. Beneficial reforms. Generally a rising stock market.

> Mars, particularly when retrograde or stationary—High death rate ; political excitement ; agrarian outrages ; strife, poverty among the farmers and humbler classes.

If the ruling sign is considered as the Ascendant of a country, then the next sign will be the second house, and so on with the other signs. Hence transits may affect each country in particular affairs according to the position of the planets from the ruling sign and also to their aspects.

In the case of towns, when the exact degree of its

ascendant and the zenith point are known, transits over these points or their opposite points cause results according to the nature of the transiting planet. Thus, Mars causes fires, accidents, assaults, epidemics. Saturn causes fall of buildings, trouble to officials, members of Councils ; city authorities and Government suffer.

Calcutta was founded by Job Charnock on the 24th August, 1690 A. D. (O. S.), at noon. The horoscope is given in page 16. Many notable events affecting this city may be found to correspond with the transits of the major planets in this horoscope. For example, on the 5th October, 1864 a violent hurricane or cyclone laid waste a great part of Calcutta, destroying nearly 200 vessels and thousands of houses and causing a loss of 70,000 lives. On this date Uranus was in the fourth house of this horoscope in square aspect with Jupiter in the ascendant and Saturn was in opposition to the place of the Moon and Jupiter was transiting the place of Saturn. Foundation of the building of the Bengal Legislative Council was laid on the 9th July, 1928, when Uranus transited the trine aspect place of the Zenith Point and of the Sun of this horoscope and also Saturn was transiting these places. On the 20th December, 1942 Calcutta was bombed by the Japanese for the first time, Uranus and Saturn were on the lower meridian and Mars was passing over the Zenith Point of this horoscope. The Great Massacre of the 16th August, 1946 is clearly indicated by the transit about this date, of Jupiter over the place of Mars in the 8th house of this horoscope, while Uranus was transiting the lower meridian in square aspect of the place of Jupiter, and on the 17th August, the central day of the Great Killing, the Moon transited the exact degree of the place of opposition of Mars.

When more than two major planets occupy a sign at the same time, the total effect is proportionately increased. A planet moving retrograde denotes an evil influence upon those men and things which are especially affected by that planet.

If during transits a planet is well aspected by other planets, the good effects are enhanced, and the evil effects modified ; but if evil aspected, the evil effects are intensified. For example, when Jupiter is transiting through a country's ruling sign and at the same time Saturn is also passing through that sign and gets an evil aspect of Uranus, the good effects of Jupiter would be affected and no apparent good will result.

Mars always produces very marked effects when near the earth, as is the case when he is retrograde. On these occasions fires are more destructive, murders are more frequent and more cruel than usual ; bloodshed is rife, and war-like deeds prevail extremely ; but these things are more obvious in those parts ruled by the sign Mars is in at the period.

Conjunctions :

The conjunctions of the superior planets Mars, Jupiter, Saturn, Uranus and Neptune at or near their perihelion, or when one of them is in aphelion, or their conjunction falls near the first point of Aries, Cancer, Libra or Capricorn, are extremely important. A horoscope is calculated for the exact time of such conjunctions. They produce effects in the countries ruled by the signs in which the conjunctions take place, or at places where the conjoined planets are exactly rising or culminating at the moment of their conjunction, and their effects last until the same two planets form their next conjunction.

> Saturn conjunction Uranus—Serious political troubles ; war ; famine ; pestilence ; earthquake.

> Jupiter conjunction Uranus—Epidemics ; strength of Government.

> Jupiter conjunction Saturn—The most important conjunction bringing political changes and serious upheavals. Mutiny, war, religious and communal disputes. When the places of other conjunctions, eclipses, and lunations, which occur after it, fall thereon, or in opposition thereto, grave effects are sure to follow.

> Mars conjunction Saturn—Government becomes unpopular and is criticised, attacked or even overthrown. War ; monarch or some important person in the state may be assassinated or may die. People discontented. Strikes, rioting, murder, inundations, storms, earthquakes.

> Mars conjunction Uranus—Similar to the conjunction with Saturn, but is more sudden

and unexpected and not so lasting. Grave political troubles. Storms.

Mars conjunction Jupiter—A crisis in business. Popular excitement, religious or communal disturbances or disputes. Law courts are full. Thunderstorms and lightning ; much heat ; earthquake.

Conjunctions of Neptune and Pluto are little understood.

Effects are greatly augmented when one of the planets is in perihelion. Also when the Sun is found with the conjunction at an eclipse or in its Ingress into Aries or other cardinal signs, the effects are augmented. But when the conjoined planets differ in latitude, the effects are greatly lessened. The periods of mutual conjunctions and oppositions of the larger planets also coincide with the periods of epidemics, earthquakes, etc., particularly when happen in Taurus and Scorpio or Cancer and Capricorn, as Taurus and Scorpio are earthquake producing signs, Cancer and Capricorn are the same, but to a less extent.

Eclipses :

The effects of eclipses are more powerful in those countries where they are actually visible, and also in those countries and cities ruled over by the sign in which the eclipse falls. The duration of the effects of a solar eclipse lasts for as many years as the eclipse is hours in length, and the influence of a lunar eclipse lasts over as many months as the eclipse is hours in duration.

Eclipses falling in Cardinal Signs : Troubles to Government and people and crops. Great mortality. Political changes and trade affected.

Eclipses falling in Fixed Signs : Sudden disasters. Troubles in national finance and money matters. Sickness, epidemics, increased death rate, death of eminent people. Earthquakes, inundations, famines, explosions, fall of buildings.

Eclipses falling in Common Signs : Labour troubles, strikes, crimes, sickness, want. Troubles connected with religion and education. Accidents in travelling.

Eclipses falling in Fiery signs : Sensational public events, disturbances, disputes, murders, danger of war, death of king or important person. Excess of heat, scarcity of rain. Increase of taxation.

Earthy signs : Damage to crops and products of the earth ; barrenness and scarcity, by reason of excessive droughts. Trade and agriculture suffer. Troublesome financial problems arise. Unfortunate for Government and statesmen. Drought.

Airy signs : Destructive storms, seditions and pestilence. Parliament suffers. Party quarrels and disputes. Disturbed relations between the nations ; questions arise relating to treaties or alliance.

> Watery signs : Excess of rain ; damage from floods ; deaths by drowning, accidents by sea or river. Sickness, danger of an epidemic. High death rate ; death of some eminent person. Labouring classes suffer and are discontent. Mysterious crimes.

In the middle of 1940 the three major planets, Uranus, Saturn and Jupiter transited the zodical sign Taurus, the second sign of the world horoscope with a great conjunction of Saturn and Jupiter opposed by Mars and Venus. This sign Taurus indicates property and produce and during the second Great World War there were great devastations and destruction of property and great dearth of food throughout the world. From this period to 1947 the Sun was either in conjunction or in evil aspect with Neptune, the planet of chaos, in all the Ingress maps. Chaos ruled in every country throughout the world. From 1948 up to 1951, the Sun will be in conjunction or in evil aspect with Uranus, the planet of revolution, in all the ingress maps, indicating great political changes and serious upheavals in all countries throughout the world. Previous conjunctions and such configurations brought also similar results, showing that Astrology has never been found wanting wherein it can be applied according to the tenets of the doctrine to indicate correctly the changes in the life and affairs of men, the birth of all nations, the coming of weather for months ahead.

PLUTO

The newly discovered Pluto plays a great part in the political and economical life of the world. Its influence is not yet fully known, but our present investigations lead to the following conclusions :

Pluto brings revolutionary upheavals, particularly when found in an angle house of Ingress Horoscopes. It brings that which has been developed under cover, in secret (underground) into daylight, when the time is ripe. It is the overthrow of the old, sensing the new. The force of Pluto is like a volcano which bubbles and seethes inside until it erupts with elementary force.

The planet indicates regeneration, reorganization, transformation, and has relationship to all that is inside and below the earth, such as caves, springs, excavations, geological as well as physical events.

All large earth movements, eruptions, geological displacements, earthquakes covering a large range, are under the influence of Pluto. It also represents all the bold and adventurous technical problems involved in stratosphere flight and the exploration of the great ocean deeps.

Pluto rules marshy districts, swamps, sections where putrescence, fermentation and putrefaction hold sway ; groves, places of worship, cemeteries, pyramids, holy shrines, borderland regions, bridges, places of horror, of destruction and of death, etc. It rules sections where, by many excavations, archaeological discoveries are made.

The countries and territories ruled by Pluto are where ancient civilizations and sunken countries are buried and submerged ; regions and localities coming within the range of volcanic activies, like Japan, New Zealand, Tierra del Fuego, Sicily, Cuba, Mexico, etc., as well as the cities of Rome, Pompeii, Messina, San Francisco, Tokyo, etc.

Pluto is pioneering, striving ahead and wants to flow from duality into oneness. He destroys the old only for the reason to be able to build up something new, or, he lets the old together but alters it, transforms it and brings forth from the elements of the old that which is new. Uranus, with its sudden seizure of more explosive forces destroys without notice, it is the unexpected and acts in a separative and destructive manner, while the destruction by Pluto wishes an amalgamation or union. The influence operates as one thing chasing the other ; events pursuing themselves ; cycles of thoughts overtaking themselves and chasing themselves. Hardly is one idea set into action, before a new one comes to the fore. Pluto tries at once to act against it, to push it ahead, and even acts as destroying, catastrophical, and does not permit things to come to rest. He brings revolutionizing political and economic struggles. The evil configurations bring about unexpected revolutions and fights bloody deeds, deeds of violence, explosions, catastrophes, unrest, sudden confusion and revolts which do not lead to a positive goal ; also sudden discoveries which do not lead to a stable end or sudden inventions which cannot be made profitable at the time. But the benefic configurations signify a very important stage in the evolution of humanity. Long buried wisdom is now unearthed, new laws, new life conditions are found and a new rhythm of life is developed. We experience inventions of an entirely new kind, which, however, bear the character of daring adventure. In this category belong the rocket problems, the stratosphere and world-space flights, the smashing of the atom, the forces of space and other fantastic problems, which can prove to be of enormous import. Likewise, there will be great progress in the realm of physics and chemistry, and the newest researches in the field of submarine life and form, in geology, and, especially, in archaelogy and medicine.

All the above have been verified since 1930, and if we study the Ingress Maps and conjunctions and aspects of Pluto with other major planets, we can easily verify the great mine disasters, traffic catastrophes, Great Second World War, great political unrest and struggle in many countries, revolutions and warlike acts in many countries, riots and massacres in India and other places, great floods and famines and economic distresses, nature-catastrophes or devastating earthquakes in Cuba, Salvador, Nicaragua, India—in all we perceive the terrible and gigantic destroying and death-bringing influence of this planet, surpassing all past records ! The so-called independence of India, Burma, downfull of Japan and Germany, loss of supremacy of the British power in the world, are all due to the influence of this planet.

CHAPTER IV

Directions in Mundane Horoscopes

There are various methods of directions used in the Quarterly, Lunation and other figures, such as 1 degree equals to 5 days, but the progression of 1 degree equivalent to 1 day seems to give better results.

These keys can be used with advantage in the Ingress figures. The key, 1 degree equivalent to 1 day, is employed in directions, which are calculated from the Right Ascensions of the Significator and Promissor.

For example : The Vernal Equinox occurred at Calcutta on the 21st March, 1946, at 11. 27 a. m. The figure is given below :

In this figure the conjunction of Mars and Saturn is only 11′ distant. According to the key 1 degree equivalent to 5 days, we find on the 22nd March, a marked fall in all share values due to this conjunction. For the conjunction of Sun and Venus there is a distance of 11° 42′. which gives 57 days, and we find about the 16th May a marked rise in the stock market. For the exact sextile between the Sun and Uranus, the difference is 13° 47′ equivalent to 78 days, which shows that about 28th May the market has a marked rise.

4

Key 1 degree equivalent to 1 day : Z. P. opposition to Neptune. The opposition of Z. P. is 19°

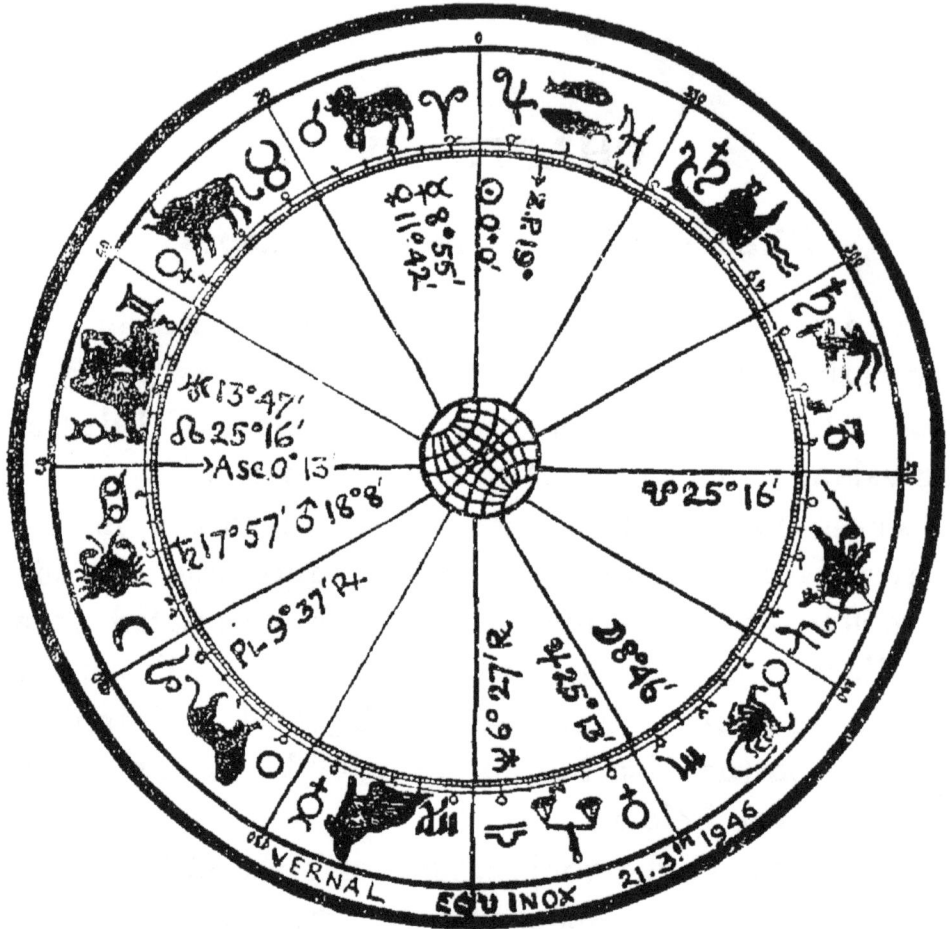

Virgo, the R.A. of which is 169° 54′, and the R.A. of Neptune is 185° 22′, the difference is 15° 28′ equivalent to 15 days. Counting from the 21st March it falls on the 5th April, on which date the market had a fall in prices. The R.A. of the Z.P. is 349° 54′ and that of the Sun is 360° The difference in the Z.P. conjunction Sun is 10° 6′ equivalent to 10 days, which counted from the 21st March, falls on the 1st April. About

this date the market had a rise. The R.A. of Saturn
is 109° 31', the square aspect of the Sun falls at 0° Cancer,
the R.A. of which is 90°   The arc of direction of Sun
square Saturn is 19° 31' equivalent to 19 days. This
counted from the 21st March falls on the 9th April,
when a fall in the market was clearly marked, but as
that was followed by Sun square Mars, the fall continued for days.

The progressions of the Z.P., Asc., Sun, and Moon
and also the cusps of the 2nd and 5th houses, direct
and converse, are to be calculated for forecasts of values.
Instead of taking the Right Ascensions, the difference
in longitudes for directional purpose may be taken,
which will also give the approximate dates. Other
progressions may be used such as directions with
Fortuna, or between the planets themselves.

In any case the period of directions must be confined within 90° or 90 days, covering the period of the
duration of the Ingress.

Also transits over the Sun and other important
planets and points in such horoscopes point out the
dates of important events and market fluctuations. In
the above map Mars came to the exact opposition to
the place of the Sun and to the conjunction of Neptune
just about the 16th August ; Mars was afflicting the
Sun at the Ingress also, the Great Calcutta Massacre
happened from the 17th to 20th August, and the market
fell afterwards to such a great ·extent as to produce
ruin to many.

CHAPTER V

Ruling Signs of Countries and Towns

There is a definite correspondence between geographical positions and celestial influence. The zodiacal rulership of a country was based by the ancient on the geological features and the kind of elemental essence flowing through it. Most of the rulerships of towns and countries given in the following list may be taken as correct, as they have been fully corroborated by experience. Still some requires further observations as great changes have taken place in modern times in Germany, Austria, Greece, Poland, Japan, etc., and in many cases large tracts of country have been incorporated from one nation with another and made them quite separate states. Also, while a country as a whole is ruled by one sign, its other parts are ruled by other signs.

The relationship of the several signs of the zodiac with the countries and chief cities of the world is thus stated by modern astrologers :—

ARIES—*Countries :* England, Germany, Denmark, Lesser Poland, Palestine, Syria, Burgundy. *Towns :* Naples, Florence, Marseilles, Cracow, Saragossa. Utrecht.

TAURUS—*Countries :* Persia, Georgia, the

Caucasus, Asia Minor, the Grecian Archipelago, Cyprus, Poland, Ireland, White Russia.

Towns   Dublin, Leipsic, Palermo, Rhodes.

GEMINI—*Countries :* Armenia, Lower Egypt, Belgium, West England, Flanders, United States of America, Wales, North-east Africa, Canada.

Towns : London (17° 54′), San Francisco, Melbourne (10° 29′), Versailles.

CANCER—*Countries :* Northen and Western Africa, Scotland, Holland, Mauritius, Paraguay.

Towns : Amesterdam, Constantinople, Genoa, Venice, Algiers, Tunis, New York (14°), Manchester (25°), Stockholm.

LEO—*Countries :* France, Italy, Sicily, Czecho-slovakia, Mesopotamia, California, Roumania,

Towns : Rome, Bristol, Bombay (25°), Chicago (5°), Damascus, Prague, Philadelphia, Portsmouth.

VIRGO—*Countries :* Turkey in Europe and Asia, Irak, Crete, Greece, West Indies, Brazil, Kurdestan, Switzerland, Virginia.

Towns : Jerusalem, Paris (14°), Boston, Los Angelos, Brindisi, Lyon, Berlin (20°), Bagdad, Corinth.

LIBRA—*Countries :* Austria, Upper Egypt, Thibet, Mongolia, Japan, Manchuria, Indo-China, Burma, Argentina.

Towns : Lisbon, Antwarp (21°), Vienna, Charles-town, Johannesburg, (27°), Copenhagen (1°).

SCORPIO—*Countries :* Morocco, Algiers, North Syria, Norway, Jutland, Bavaria, West Sweden, Queensland, Lappland, Transvaal,

Towns : Liverpool, Messina (18°), Baltimore, Cincinnati, Dover, Newfoundland (2°), Newcastle, New Orleans, Washington, Munich, Baden-Baden.

SAGITTARIUS—*Countries :* Spain, Australia, Madagascar, Arabia, Hungary, Slavonia, Moravia, Part of France between La Seine and La Garonne to Cape Finisterre.

Towns : Calcutta (2°), Peking (16°), Budapest.

CAPRICORN—*Countries :* India, Afghanistan, the Punjab, Mexico, South Africa, Bulgaria, Albania, Jugoslavia.

Towns : Tokyo (7°), Brussels, Oxford, Port Said, Dresden, Moscow, Warshaw.

AQUARIUS—*Countries :* Arabia, Red Russia, Prussia, part of Poland, Lithuania, Sweden, Abyssinia, Finland. *Towns :* Sidney (10°), Hamburg, Brighton.

PISCES—*Countries :* Portugal, Calabria, Normandy, Galicia, Nubia, Sahara, Sicily, Malta, St. Helena, Cape of Good Hope, South of Asia Minor, Ceylon, Batavia.

Towns : Alexandria, Calcutta (5°).

The sign ruling a town is generally ascertained by noting the hour and minute of the occurrence of important events, laying foundation stones, opening buildings, beginning public ceremonies, and other affairs that influence the community as a whole or a considerable portion of it. At such times one particular zodiacal sign will be found to rise oftener than others, which is considered as the ruling sign of the concerned town.

Many years ago Albert Ross Parsons used the great

Pyramid of Gizeh as the starting point from which to co-ordinate geographic longitude with zodiacal longitude, and thus obtain the sign and degree ruling each place on the earth's surface according to its longitude. A few years ago L. Edward Johndro also took the pyramidal data but considered that the longitude gradually shifts due to the precession of equinoxes. Quite recently Paul Counsil also tried the same thing but taking the Pyramid of Cheops as the starting point and shifting the longitude according to the precession from the fixed star Aldebaran. Johndro fixed the 0° Aries at 29° 10' west lengitude, for 1930, while according to Counsil it falls at 36° 42' west longitude.

Sepharial in his "Theory of Geodetic Equivalents" assumes that 0 degree longitude on the earth's surface from the meridian of Greenwich corresponds to 0 degree Aries on the ecliptic, that 30 degrees east longitude on the earth's surface corresponds to 0 degree Taurus, and so on. These correspondences are for the Zenith Points of the localities. The ascendant is therefore found from a Table of Houses for the latitude of the place for this Zenith Point. Thus, in Lat. 22° 33' N. and Long. 88° 22' E., which defines the city of Calcutta, the Zenith Point is 28° 22' Gemini and 28° 19' Virgo is the Ascendant. Similarly, Bombay, Lat. 18° 54' N., Long. 72° 49' E. has the Zenith Point as 12° 49' Gemini and 12° 22' Virgo as the Ascendant. Delhi, Lat. 28° 30' N., Long. 77° 15' E. has 17° 15' Gemini as the Zenith Point and 17° 48' Virgo as the Ascendant. Madras, Lat. 13° 4' N., Long. 80° 14' E. has 20° 14'

Gemini as the Zenith Point and 19° 28′ Virgo, Ascendant. It thus appears that India is chiefly ruled by Virgo.

Sepharial's efforts to establish the co-ordinates between each area of the earth and its celestial correspondence are well worth studying as many striking results have been found from this method.

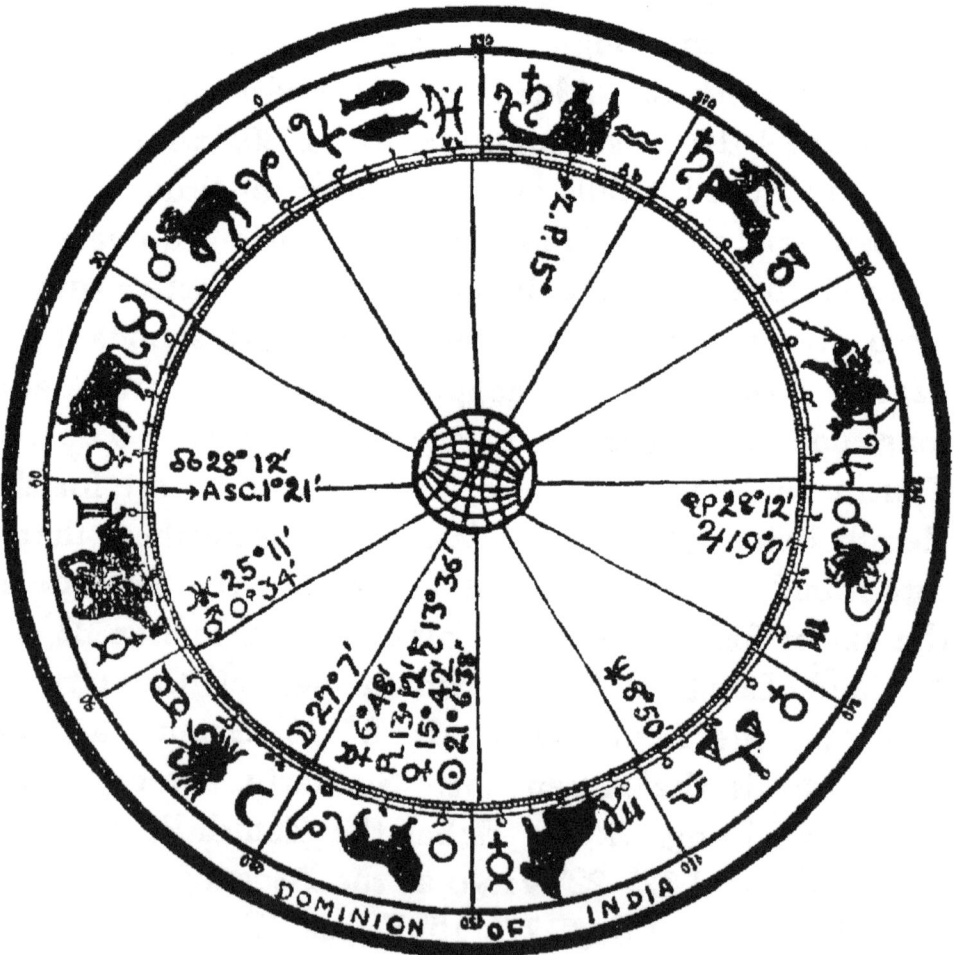

DOMINION OF INDIA

CHAPTER VI

Planets in the Signs of the Zodiac

The transits of the major planets through the signs of the zodiac and when they form important aspects therein, or an eclipse falls in those signs, invariably coincide with big events affecting the stocks and shares in the countries ruled by such signs. The planets moving in a sign also affects the country ruled by the decanate in which they are placed.

A list of the ruling signs of countries has been given in the previous chapter. The signs indicated by the decanates of each sign are given below, from which the countries ruled by the decanates may be easily ascertained.

Sign	Aries	Taurus	Gemini	Cancer	Leo	Virgo
Decanate I	Aries	Taurus	Gemini	Cancer	Leo	Virgo
Decanate II	Leo	Virgo	Libra	Scorpio	Sagitt.	Capricorn
Decanate III	Sagitt.	Capric.	Aquar.	Pisces	Aries	Taurus

Sign	Libra	Scorpio	Sagitt.	Capricorn	Aquarius	Pisces
Decanate I	Libra	Scorpio	Sagitt.	Capric.	Aquar.	Pisces
Decanate II	Aquar.	Pisces	Aries	Taurus	Gemini	Cancer
Decanate III	Gemini	Cancer	Leo	Virgo	Libra	Scorpio

All these transits are to be interpreted in terms of the last major conjunction of the planet in that sign. For if the indications are of depressions, the fortunes of that country ruled by the sign will be accordingly depressed and no good aspects of the transiting planet will do more than a temporary improvement, but evil aspects will bring more evil.

Benefics and Moon's North Node transiting the ruling sign of a country unless there are other secondary unfavourable signs, will bring a good rise. When transiting in the opposite signs, they will generally cause a fall.

Jupiter shows expansion, prosperity and advancing prices. The conjunction of Mars and Jupiter in the ruling sign of a country brings great fluctuations in prices, a crisis in highly speculative buying. The conjunction of Jupiter and Saturn brings steady advances in values and that with Uranus, prosperity and advancement in price, new enterprises and financial revisions and reconstructions and reforms. The conjunction of Neptune does not have a sufficiently marked influence on the market.

Saturn causes a depression and its conjunction with Mars causes depression. The conjunction of Saturn and Uranus brings changes and depressions in prices, while the conjunction of Neptune does not show any outstanding effects. Mars and Neptune in conjunction also do not produce any marked effect.

The conjunction of Uranus and Neptune makes a departure of a new cycle of moral, social and industrial organization ; good, if it receives good aspects. But generally unsound finance and inflationary scheme with a period of prosperity and progress of political and economic condition are indicated. With evil aspects, political and economic disorders and chaos are shown.

The evil effects of a conjunction is lessened if it occurs in a sign, that is the house of exaltation of one of the two planets, or if there is much difference of latitude between them ; but the effect is increased, if the sign is the detrement or fall of either.

The passage of the major planets in the ruling sign of a country or its opposite sign affects the prices of the Government Securities of that country. Thus, in 1914 and 1915 when Saturn passed through Cancer, the opposite sign ruling India, the prices of Government Securities fell considerably. Also in 1920-21 when Saturn passed through Virgo, also considered as the ruling sign of India, the prices of the Securities were very low. Again in 1925 when Saturn passed through the sign Capricorn, the price was low. In 1944 and 1945 Jupiter was passing through Virgo and the prices of the Government Securities were higher. Generally the aspects of the Sun are to be noted for the market tone of these securities, as they indicate very closely the state of the Government of the country whose sign the Sun is in at the time. These should be considered along with the aspects of the major planets.

From the above it will be evident that no set of

circumstances could cause all the stocks in geographically distributed investment list to show a simultaneous depreciation. An investor who geographically distributes his capital can, with safety, afford to hold stocks which yield a larger income than he can hope to receive from an investment list which disregards the important point of geographical distribution.

Not only do wars, political troubles, trade stagnation or prosperity influence the prosperity of the enterprises and the prices of stocks which are held in a country, but such events as these also affect the stocks in which that individual country is the dominant market. This is a point which should be most carefully considered by all those who desire to obtain a real international distribution of risks.

CHAPTER VII

General Significators of Commodities

The planets and the signs of the zodiac have rule over certain kinds of commodities and stocks and industries. For the general consideration of the price condition of a commodity or stock, the disposition and aspects of the planet or sign ruling it should be considered.

The SUN represents the Government stocks and gilt-edged securities. Gold, precious stones, rice, honey, aromatic herbs as need for flavouring.

The MOON is not a particular indicator for any commodity. It is said to rule milk. It is also considered to have some influence in industrials and commercial undertakings; petroleum shares, hotel and catering concerns; brewery, oil shares in general; liquids (such as wines but also those trades dependent upon liquids); navigation, fishery; silver, glass; mushroom, lettuce, watercress, cabbage, melon, cucumber, pumpkin, turnip, ghee.

When connected with Mars—oil industries; with Venus—cosmetic oils; with Jupiter—salad oils.

MERCURY rules schools, trade shares, publishing

business, newspaper, publicity ; railways communication ; cotton production, jute ; silver, quicksilver ; carrots, parsley, groundnut, the majority of nuts.

When connected with Saturn—mercury industry ; paper industry.

VENUS rules sugar prices, cotton prices, jute prices, wheat prices ; hessian, silk and textile industry ; sugar industry and shares, confectionery ; pearl industry ; mirror and glass industry ; flower cultivation ; copper, copper trade and industry ; fancy articles industry ; catering mainly for women ; perfumery industry ; apple, pear, vine, gooseberry and other berries. Most of the spices.

MARS rules iron and steel industry ; sugar produce and supply ; rice market ; railways shares ; all metal industries and those dependent primarily upon machinary ; constructional industries (buildings) ; those dependent upon iron and fire (munition) ; brick manufactory ; distillery·; coffee, tea ; practically all 'hot' foods, such as ginger and those of strong taste, such as, onion, garlic, etc.

JUPITER rules banks, religious, legal and financial concerns ; cloth mills ; food stuffs and luxury trade ; cocoa, grams, etc. Rubber, tin, zinc, tobacco, gas.

Bank difficulties generally arise when Jupiter passes through Gemini, Virgo, Scorpio, Capricorn and Aquarius. Failures are ·mostly liable to occur when Jupiter is retrograde in these signs. When Jupiter passes through Sagittarius, all banks do well.

SATURN rules mining, farming and cement works ;

building concerns ; shoe factory ; real estates ; mines, agriculture ; metallurgy, lead, coal, marble, quarry ; jute ; barley ; most vegetables such as potato, parsnip, spinach.

URANUS rules aerial and electrical industries, wireless and telegraph, aerial navigation, motor cars industries, railroads, tramways, buses ; public or state railway shares, Government papers ; Joint Stock Companies, associates, etc. ; film industries ; aerated water industry ; aeroplanes ; aluminium, amalgams of metals ; hessian. The more modern departures in industries ; highly speculative ventures of things of a novel character.

NEPTUNE rules oil and fishing industries ; India-rubber and caoutchouc industry : synthetic manufactures such as, artificial silk, etc. Narcotics, opium, tobacco ; drugs ; petrol, oils ; raw cotton,

The influence of PLUTO is not sufficiently known to be classified in this manner.

ARIES rules rails, machinary, iron, steel, rice.

TAURUS rules sugar value, molasses, wheat, cotton, jute, textiles, medicine. General share values.

GEMINI rules railways, trams, buses ; paper, publication, newspaper, jute and raw cotton.

CANCER rules silver, tea.

LEO rules gold; currency, Government stocks.

VIRGO rules cotton crops, corn ; clothing ; labour condition.

LIBRA rules cotton price, jute, wheat price, grain, food stuff.

SCORPIO rules oils, chemicals, petroleum, oil seeds like linseed, groundnut, mustard, cotton seed.

SAGITTARIUS rules tin, rubber, zinc.

CAPRICORN rules coal, lead, mining shares.

AQUARIUS rules electricity, electrical goods, silk, hessian.

PISCES rules fishery, brewery, oils, river, canal.

Cardinal signs rule industrial and commercial undertakings. Fixed signs, gilt-edged securities, Government stocks, etc. Common signs generally rule international stocks, etc. Fiery signs rule gas and lighting, chemical stocks. Earthy signs, wheat, coal, collieries. Airy signs rule aeroplanes, wireless, telegraph, etc. Watery signs rule river and canal.

The Steel stocks as a group come under the rulership of earthy and watery signs ; the Oil stocks come under the influence of the airy signs, particlularly Libra ; the Chemical stocks come under the fiery signs ; the Utilities come under a combination of watery and earthy signs. Whenever the Sun or other major planets pass through these signs, stocks which fall under these groups are stimulated to activity.

Transits of major planets in several signs of the zodiac affect the price of commodities and shares indicated by them, according to the nature and aspects of the planets. Jupiter brings a rise and Saturn, a depression. A retrograde planet affects rather strongly.

Transits in Aries affect the price of crops and all agricultural products, share markets as well as bullion market to some extent.

Transits in Taurus affect cotton and bullion markets.

Transits in Gemini show a general bearish or bullish tendency with sporadic rises in all markets or falls according to the nature and aspects of the planets.

Transits in Cancer affect trade activities, industries with much speculative tendencies in shares and bullion markets.

Transits in Leo affect the values of farm products, grain, metals and bullion. Textiles and Jute are depressed while Steel and engineering concerns show activities.

Transits in Virgo affect generally crops and earthly products, cotton, wheat.

Transits in Libra affect cotton and general share values.

Transits in Scorpio affect oils, oil shares, medicine and drugs.

Transits in Sagittarius affect rubber and metals.

Transits in Capricorn affect mine shares and bullion market.

Transits in Aquarius affect silk, cotton, metals.

Transits in Pisces affect the general market.

CHAPTER VIII

Astrological Principles in Market Forecasting

The art of stock speculation is not a simple affair and comes somewhat differently than what the speculator thinks or desires. The general advice is : Buy before a rise in value ; sell before a fall. This golden rule has an admirable sound ; but it is futile unless it is capable of being embodied in some practical workable shape. Can, then, some pertinent interpretation be devised by which one can detect with remarkable exactness, the point when the possibly highest ascent has been attained, or is being attained, with the consequent time for sale and the approximately extreme depression, which suggests the advantage of purchase ? In these matters astrology can help beneficially, when reason and moderation are the guiding principle. Of course, the look-out for the lowest fall and the highest rise is dangerous and should be avoided, for, thereby the speculator generally gets the worse business. Also one should never speculate with all the money he can command, but shall lay out a separate fund for speculation, or when the means thereto does not suffice, may risk only a portion of his property.

When one speculates according to astrological principles, he should implicitly follow the rules, although at times perhaps more advantages may be obtained by not too strictly following the rules but at the same time there may be risk of loss without following them. Thus, for example, when a date is considered from planetary configurations as giving the lowest value for purchase, but actually the lowest value occurs two or three days after. But there should be no ground to be sorry for this, for one should follow a principle systematically and faithfully to obtain sure result and be on the safe side. Similarly, suppose from astrological considerations, we find that a particular date is good for purchase and when actually the price is found to be the lowest, but unexpectedly the price rises within a few days after this and thus brings a gain. Here if one wait for further fall in price, he will suffer loss and get the worse. But with the astrological principles there would be a sure method of gain without much risk, although the maximum advantage may not be obtained.

Another fundamental rule is : Purchase often and sell often ; to be satisfied with small profits, for many small profits make a big one. But in spite of this, there will be occasions when it will be profitable to take recourse to long term speculation, particularly in dealing with stocks of different countries or kinds of concerns.

From the consideration of the general planetary configurations and also their positions and aspects in the Mundane Horoscopes and their transits through the concerning houses (particularly the second house) in the political horoscope of a particular country or a chief business town, the condition of the money market of that place may be ascertained with fair accuracy.

Though the monthly trend of price fluctuations can be ascertained with fair accuracy according to the above mundane figures, the daily fluctuations cannot be exactly ascertained from them. The general tendency of rise and fall in the stock and share market depends ordinarily on the planetary positions and configurations in the quarterly and lunation figures.

The finance of the State may be judged from the quarterly and lunation figures. From the maps of eclipses or of the conjunctions of major planets, the financial state may also be judged, but not in a general manner, except only when a crisis is expected. Conjunctions of the major planets coincide with the greatest troubles in the country whose sign they occur in. A conjunction of Saturn and Uranus is a sure signal of widespread distress, usually famine and epidemics. Oppositions operate in much the same manner. The conjunction of Jupiter and Saturn causes great political changes like the serious political troubles caused by the conjunction of Saturn and Uranus. The conjunction of Saturn and Mars indicates unpopularity of the Government, strikes and riots. A conjunction of Jupiter and Uranus is often followed by epidemics, but it brings strength to the Government. A conjunction of Jupiter and Mars produce popular excitement, communal disturbances and a crisis in the market. A conjunction of Mars and Uranus generally produces sudden and unexpected grave political troubles. The conjunction with Neptune or Pluto are very little understood, but generally they portend evil. Generally the countries ruled by the sign in which the conjunction happens, are affected, but not to an equal extent in all such countries. The parts of the world where it is angular feel its greatest effect.

Concerning the mundane figures, it must be noted that the financial condition of a State or Government, the economic condition of the Government may be judged from them. The values of stocks and shares or industrials are affected indirectly and are to be judged also from other planetary configurations, but the general tendency is shown by the financial condition of the Government, for, when the Government Stocks improve there will be rise in all other stocks. Also when one kind of stocks declines or advances in value, other stocks frequently show a similar tendency without any apparent cause.

From the general planetary configurations in the quarterly Ingress maps with reference to the basic mundane horoscope of the concerned country or its chief town, the fluctuations of values may be ascertained and in which the planetary transits in certain particular houses, especially the second, occur, will show the course.

The horoscopes of some of the principal financial centres are given below :

Town	Ascendant	Zenith Point
Berlin	Virgo 24°	Gemini 22°
Bombay	Scorpio 2°	Leo 22°
Calcutta	Sagittarius 2° also Pisces 5°	Virgo 7° also Sagittarius 5°
Copenhagen	Libra 10°	Cancer 10°
London	Gemini 17° 54'	Aquarius 12° 3
New Orleans	Gemini 27°	Pisces 3°
New York	Cancer 14°	Pisces 24°
Paris	Virgo 14°	Gemini 11°
Peking	Sagittarius 16°	Libra 6°
Rome	Virgo 23°	Gemini 22°
Tokyo	Capricorn 7°	Libra 29°

We can find the dates of fluctuations in the market of a country from directions and transits of the planets in the quarterly, lunation and other mundane figures, particularly in the second house. High and remarkable fluctuations are generally observed during war times and in times of crises in a country, but in other times moderate fluctuations are shown.

Also for this purpose special attention is to be paid to the conjunctions and oppositions of the major planets falling over the important places in the charts of various countries or towns and also in the Ingress or other maps.

The planets show the tendency of a rise or a fall, but a comparison whether the rise or fall in one period is greater or lesser than another is not possible. When the value of a stock or commodity is very low the daily fluctuations may be marked with fair accuracy from the consideration of planetary influences. Also when the value rules very high the daily fluctuations may be noted with accuracy in some measure, but such is not the case when the value is moderately high or low. Here we can accurately judge the monthly course of the value and determine the critical month in which the tendency will be either towards a rise or towards a fall.

The planets affect the market according to the aspects they receive. It may be fairly safely taken that trade generally is at a low ebb during the adverse aspects, and correspondingly high during the benefic aspects.

The individual planet affects the market in the following manner :

MERCURY shows a nervous market, and when in evil aspect, instability and rapid fluctuations, particularly the shares ruled by it tend to decline.

VENUS gives a steady tendency, but when in evil aspect, deplorable state of inactivity.

MARS shows the movements to be brisk and sharp, favourable or unfavourable according to the nature of the aspect, particularly when Jupiter is in any way connected.

JUPITER shows expansion and rise, even its evil aspects are not very unfavourable.

SATURN shows fall when in evil aspect ; but well aspected, makes the market stable and steady.

URANUS shows unexpected rise and fall. Good aspects show sudden rises and evil aspects, falls.

NEPTUNE shows queer movements and chaos in the market; overactivity in speculative shares; deceptive tone in the market.

The inflation periods are, when

1. Jupiter is in conjunction with Uranus in the summer Ingress map.
2. Jupiter is in the first or second house of a country's or town's or of its Stock Exchange Horoscope.
3. Jupiter is in the ruling sign of a country.
4. Jupiter is in conjunction with Moon's North Node, or in sextile or trine aspect with Saturn or Uranus. ⟁
5. Saturn is in a benefic aspect with Uranus.

The depression periods are, when

1. Saturn is in the second house of a country's or town's or of its Stock Exchange Horoscope.
2. Saturn transits the ruling sign of a country.
3. Saturn is in conjunction with or in evil aspect with the Moon's North Node.
4. Saturn is in conjunction or in evil aspect with Uranus.
5. Uranus is in conjunction or in evil aspect with the Moon's North Node.

CHAPTER IX

General Considerations

When we consider the financial condition of a particular country or state in relation to that of the other countries or states, we find great divergencies between them according to the standard of living and political situation of these particular countries. The Mundane Horoscopes from the Ingress of the Sun into cardinal signs and from the Lunation Figures are, however, not the only deciding factors indicative of such conditions. There are other factors such as transits of the superior planets in the ruling sign of the concerned country, eclipses falling in such sign, figures erected for the moments of conjunctions of the major planets, such as, Jupiter and Saturn, Jupiter and Uranus, Jupiter and Mars, and Saturn and Uranus, and also the configurations in such horoscopes by other planets from transits. The mundane horoscopes indicate the general tendency of the fluctuations of the Money Market, Stocks and Shares, or of commodities, but to find out accurately the rise and fall of values, one must consider all the above-mentioned factors in respect of a particular country or state from its political horoscope,

that is, from the horoscope of its political foundation
or from the horoscope of the Stock Exchange of its
important business centres.   Thus, the political horoscope of India was taken for the 1st November, 1858,
noon, Allahabad, the date when India was declared
as a British Empire. But the political horoscope is
now to be taken for 0 a. m., on the 15th August,
1947, when both the Indian and Pakistan Dominions
have been born.   (See   horoscope in page 56).
The political horoscope of Turkey is at present
calculated for noon, 29th October, 1922 at Ankara.
The political horoscope of Great Britain is calculated
for noon, 8th May, 1660, London. The political
horoscope of Russia is calculated for noon, 30th
December, 1922, Moscow ; that of Sweden, at
noon, 17th June, 1523, Stockholm. The political
horoscope of Spain is cast for noon, 14th April, 1931,
Madrid, and that of Canada, for noon, 22nd May, 1867,
Quebec ; of Mexico, noon, 16th December, 1823. The
political horoscope of United States of America is
cast for noon, 4th July, 1776, Philadelphia, and that of
Australia, for noon, 9th July, 1900 ; of China, noon,
12th February, 1912, Nanking ; of Burma, 3-15 a. m.,
4th January, 1948, Rangoon ; of Portugal, noon, 4th
October, 1910, Lisbon ; of Norway, 6 p. m., 13th
August, 1905, Oslo. The previous political horoscope
before the Second Great World War, of Italy was
8 p. m., 29th October, 1922, Rome ; of Germany,
for 12. 15 p. m, 30th January, 1933, Berlin ; of France,
for 4.45 p. m., 4th September, 1870, Paris ; of Greece,

for noon, 28th February, 1924, Athens ; of Japan, noon, 11th February, 1889, Tokyo. The new political horoscopes for these countries would have to be cast for the dates of their newly formed Governments after the Second Great World War.

The Money Market always remains in direct connection with the national economy and the financial condition of a State or Government. For the judgment of the general condition of the Money Market, we have therefore to consider the political horoscope of a country and also the quarterly figures of the Sun's entries into the cardinal signs, and for the particular fluctuations, the lunation figures of each month. The solar Ingress figures act as the hour hand and the Lunation figures as the minute hand so to speak. Further, the consideration of the maps of eclipses and great conjunctions from the daily transits of the superior planets over the sensitive places of these horoscopes also helps in this direction.

The political horoscope of a country, that is, the map of an important political reform in the Government of a country, may be useful for ascertaining the economical condition of a country from directions and transits in the map, but for general market forecasting it is of little value and consequently is not treated here.

The Ingress and other mundane figures generally show the economical conditions which stay in direct connection with the finance of the State. These conditions chiefly affect the values of stocks and shares, and the ups and downs in the values can be judged from the configurations formed by the progressions and transits of the planets in these horoscopes, and also by the aspects formed by the planets among themselves by their daily movements. These charts must be calculated for the latitude and longitude of the place which is the recognized centre for dealing in stocks and shares or for commercial dealings in a commodity, the market fluctuations for which is required to be ascertained, though for judging the political affairs of a country, the charts are calculated for the capital cities of the Government of a country or State. Thus, we take London for Stocks and Shares and Railway Markets of Britain, New York for Wall Street, New Orleans for American Cotton Market, Bombay for Indian Stock and Share Market as well as for Cotton ; Calcutta also for Stock and Share Market as well as for Jute and Tea Markets. For particular subjects we have to select particular places, such as, Chicago for the potted Meat Industry, Johannesburg for the Rand Gold Mines, Buenos Ayres for Argentine, and Odessa for Russian Wheat ; Calcutta for Jute, etc. The principal maps required are those of the Ingresses or entries of the Sun into Aries, Cancer, Libra and Capricorn, added to these the Lunation nearest the Vernal Equinox and also the maps for eclipses *when visible at the places for which they are calculated*, besides the maps of the heavens for the time of great conjunctions of the major planets, such as, Mars or Jupiter with Saturn, Uranus, and so on.

For the consideration of the condition of the Money Market of a country get all the Mundane Maps of the heavens for the place of operation with the data of transits and lunations affecting the same.

The specific house indications in respect of the Money Market are :

The First House governs the public in which is vested all forms of enterprise and development.

The Second House relates to the price of money, trade returns, bullion imports, bills of exchange, etc. Banks, Government revenues, rise and fall of national property. Rates, taxes.

The first and second houses represent "Bulls". In stock market "Bull" signifies one who purchases what he does not require. He estimates or reasons valid to himself that the value of a particular stock is likely to rise, and desires, when that event occurs, to be in a position to avail himself of the chance of selling ; but in order to gain this position he must obviously first purchase.

The Third House rules railroads, tramways, omnibus, traction of all sorts, locomotion, telephone, aircraft, canals, bridges and transports such as, postal services and all means of communication. Stocks and shares of a country.

The Fourth House rules real estate, land, exploration, mines, developments, crops, produce of raw material from the soil.

The Fifth House shows educational matters, art, theatres, cinemas, amusements and schools.

The Sixth House governs foodstuffs, clothing, equipment, outfitting, supplies, upholstering, furnishing, building and uplifting.

The Seventh House rules accountancy, banking corporation, exchanges, contracts, equity, surveying, valuation, etc.

The Eighth House controls waste products, conservancy, dredging, petrol, paraffin, benzine, medical accessories, chemicals and nitrates. Death duties.

The Seventh and Eighth houses indicate "Bears". A "Bear" sells what he does not possess. He surmises that the price of a special stock will probably fall ; if he can sell now at a certain price and his anticipation of a decline be realized, he can then, by purchasing the stock at the reduced value secure the profit between the price at which he originally sold and the diminished price at which he can now buy, and thus complete his bargain by a successful delivery. Hence. in order to occupy the position of an advantageous purchaser when the price declines, he effects a present speculative sale.

The Ninth House is connected with insurance, cables, publishing, wireless, radiographs, telegraphs, liners, foreign affairs. Commercial power of the country.

The Tenth House rules state affairs ; the Government and political activity generally.

The Eleventh House is related to Exchequer Bonds, Government Loans, Electric and Gaslight Companies ; irrigation, museums, guilt-edged securities, syndicates.

The Twelfth House rules laundries, breweries, fisheries, boot manufacture, hosiery, cold storage.

The Ingresses, Lunations, Conjunctions of the major planets, Eclipses, etc., all have their significance according to the house of the horoscope in which they occur or are related to them cosmically.

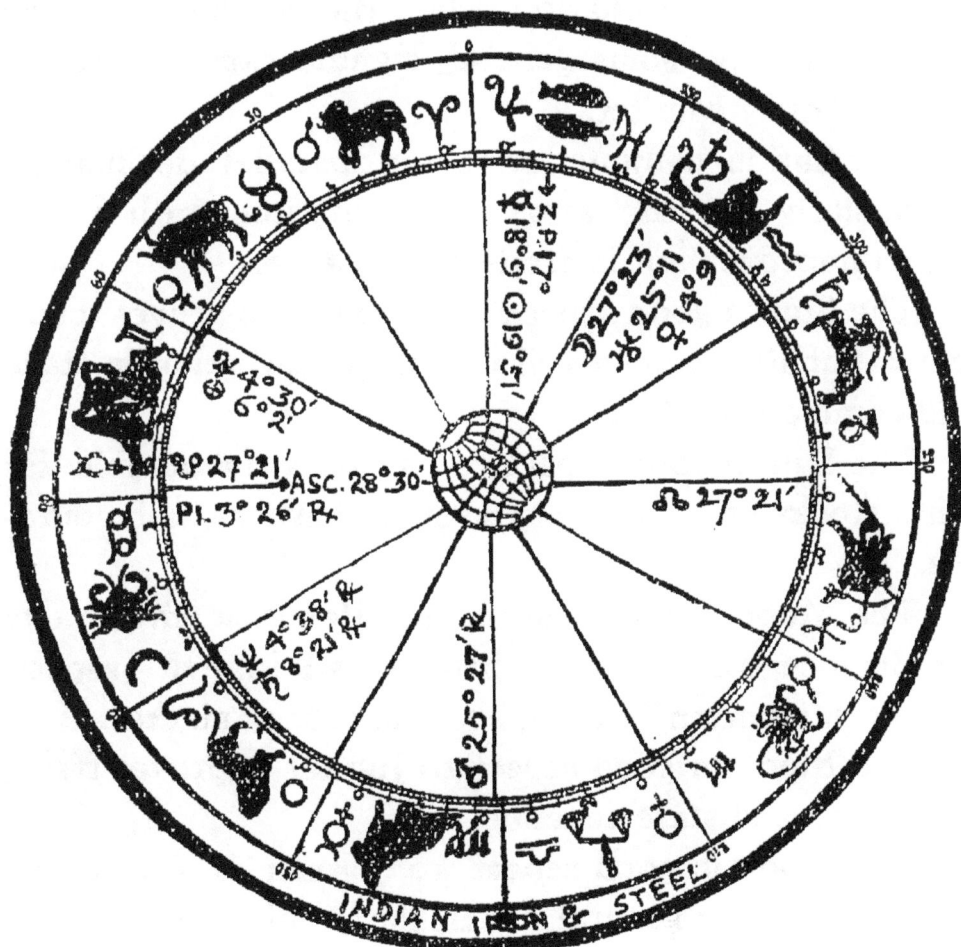

INDIAN IRON & STEEL

CHAPTER X

General Significations

In an Ingress or Lunation Map the aspects between the planets have some general signification in respect of the Money Market.

The Sun in conjunction or in parallel declination, particularly of the same denomination, with Venus shows improvement in trade and finance.

The Sun in good aspect to Jupiter improves commercial affairs ; but in evil aspect, perturbation in trade and commercial affairs.

The Sun in good aspect to Saturn is favourable for mine stocks and shares ; and in evil aspect, unfavourable.

The Moon in good aspect to Venus is favourable for finance and general prosperity ; in evil aspect, causes fluctuation in exchange and money market.

The Moon in good aspect to Jupiter improves trade, commerce and state revenue.

The Moon in good aspect to Saturn is favourable for the stocks in general, particularly mines stocks and shares. The evil aspect is not good for trade, causes fluctuations in values of stocks and shares, particularly of mines.

Mercury in good aspect to Jupiter is good for trade and commercial affairs, its evil aspect is unfavourable.

Venus in good aspect to Mars is favourable for money market and internal and foreign trade, while its evil aspect brings perturbation in the money market.

Venus in good aspect to Saturn is favourable for commercial affairs, stocks and shares and general trade conditions. The evil aspect is unfavourable for money affairs and commerce ; it signifies loss or defect in the public revenue, depreciation of stocks. Banks and trade concerns are not prosperous at this time.

Venus in good aspect to Uranus is generally favourable for money market and its evil aspect is unfavourable.

Mars in evil aspect with Jupiter is unfavourable for the money market. It generally brings a commercial crisis or a fall in the stock market.

Jupiter in good aspect to Saturn is favourable for the Government revenue ; for trade and commerce ; steadiness in prices of stocks and shares. An evil aspect is unfavourable for Government revenue and brings a critical period in the money market, in trade and commerce, and banks, and a fall in values of stocks and shares.

FIRST HOUSE

When the Moon passes through the first house and is well placed and obtains good aspects, its effects on

6

the money market are favourable. But when the Moon is badly placed and in evil aspects, contrary will be the effects.

Mercury influences in like manner with particular relation to trade and industry.

Venus and Jupiter well placed in the first house and receiving good aspects work favourably. But their evil aspects are not seriously evil.

Badly placed Saturn, Uranus or Neptune and in evil aspects in this house works unfavourably, while good aspects show moderately favourable effects.

Generally the condition and occupation of the four cardinal houses of the horoscope by planets determine the nature of the effects. When a house is unoccupied, judgment should be made from the position and aspects of its ruler.

SECOND HOUSE

Sun in this house and in good aspects brings good results and advancement in the values. With evil aspects the contrary is signified.

Lunation falling in this house, if well aspected, indicates prosperous time for stocks and shares, particularly gilt-edged securities. If badly aspected, bank failures, losses on the Stock Exchange may be expected.

The Moon in the second house causes fluctuation in the market. By good aspects, a rise in the value of stocks and shares, favourable advancement in prices of commodities and new source of revenues of the Government are indicated. By evil aspects, financial crisis, loss, fall in values of stocks and shares are shown.

Mercury in the second, well placed and well aspected, works favourably on affairs ruled by it. By evil position and aspects, it works unfavourably and causes fall in values of stocks. Good deal of sharp practice in the money market is shown.

Venus in the second house is generally favourable. By unfavourable position and aspects, it gives fluctuations of values of stocks and shares, also is bad for banks and commercial affairs.

Mars in this house generally shows losses on the Stock Exchange, panics, bank troubles. But if well placed and well aspected, it improves the financial condition of the State and acts favourably in the matters ruled by it. With evil position and aspects, it causes speculation fever, a sudden fall in the market, loss on the Stock Exchange, run on banks.

Jupiter well placed and in good aspects in the second, indicates much improvement in the money market, improvement in banking and commercial affairs. The price of gold advances and there is a general rise in stock values. By its evil position and aspects, anxiety in the money market, panics on the Stock Exchange and bank troubles are shown. If the evil aspect comes from Saturn, great depression and fall in prices, and loss for banks, etc., are shown. Evil aspects from Mars cause crises and fall in share values.

Saturn in the second in evil position and aspects, indicates fall in the values of stocks and securities.

Banks and money market suffer under depression. But if Saturn is here well placed and receives very good aspects, steady tone of the market and in values of securities is shown. When Saturn has got neutral or no aspects, financial crises, stagnation and depression are shown.

Uranus in the second in a favourable position and well aspected, brings a sudden rise in the values of stocks and shares, improvement in the finance of the State and in exchange value. In unfavourable sign and in evil aspects, it brings sudden falls and great crises and fluctuations in the money market, bank failures and fall in the values of stocks and shares. Strange and unlooked-for occurrences may be expected on the Stock Exchange.

Neptune in the second in evil aspects works unfavourably.

When the house is unoccupied, judgment should be made from the position and aspects of its ruler.

THIRD HOUSE

The evil aspected Mars or Uranus in the third house threatens depreciation of values of railways shares or traffic concerns. Contrary is shown by a well aspected Jupiter or Uranus in this house.

The evil aspected Saturn in the third brings retrogression in the money market.

The other planets generally affect the railways shares according to the good or evil aspects they recieve in this house. Zadkiel predicted rise and fall with bewildering effects in the American Railways Stocks from the Moon in the third house in square to Jupiter and Saturn and in parallel declination to Mercury from a Vernal Ingress Map for Washington.

FOURTH HOUSE

The Fourth House of an Ingress figure will give much information about the condition of crops and the probable weather conditions affecting them during the ensuing quarter. This house also relates to the stocks and shares connected with agriculture, mines and forests, collieries and coal.

Lunation falling in this house will affect the matters governed thereby favourably or unfavourably according to the good or evil aspects received.

The well aspected Sun or Moon in this house causes good progress in mines and agricultural shares. If evil aspected, the reverse is shown.

Mercury in the fourth with good aspects brings rise and improvement in agricultural and mining shares. Evil aspects bring the opposite. But this position of Mercury is not very important.

Venus in this house is favourable or unfavourable according to its good or evil aspects, but is not very important.

Mars in this house shows troubles affecting land and agriculture generally. The landed property will suffer. If afflicted, the evil is augmented.

Jupiter in good aspects in the fourth house brings much improvement in agricultural and mining concerns and enhancement in the values of such shares. The evil aspects are not of much importance.

Saturn in the fourth causes particularly when in evil aspects, depression of values of land and soil, especially product of agriculture would suffer under it. Also it indicates depression in the money market.

Uranus and Neptune often brings sudden changes and fluctuations according to their aspects and nature. They bring troubles to land and mining concerns.

SEVENTH HOUSE

Evil aspected Jupiter, Saturn, Uranus or Neptune generally brings perturbation in foreign trade and financial affairs.

TENTH HOUSE

Evil aspected Jupiter and other major planets generally bring weakness in the Government finance.

ELEVENTH HOUSE

Jupiter in this house, particularly if well aspected, shows progress in all affairs concerned with trade and finance. But if evil aspected, it will bring depreciation of Government securities. Saturn, Uranus and Neptune are generally evil in this house.

The other houses are not of much importance in judging market conditions.

GREAT CONJUNCTIONS

The great conjunctions and oppositions between Jupiter and Mars show great financial perturbations. The same happen from the opposition and square aspects between Jupiter and Saturn, Jupiter and Uranus and Saturn and Uranus.

A conjunction of Mars and Jupiter on the 24th September, 1946 fell on the fifth house of the Autumn Ingress figure for Calcutta, which indicated bank crisis and heavy fall on the Stock Exchange.

LUNATIONS AND ECLIPSES

Lunations (New Moons and sometimes Full Moons, which, however, are inferior in importance to New Moons, except when they are eclipses) falling in a particular house of the Ingress horoscope affect the affairs of the house. In financial affairs the second, fourth and the tenth houses have much significance. The influence of a New Moon extends until the next New Moon.

A Lunation in the second house causes general fluctuations in the money market. By good aspects, advance in values of stocks and shares, improvement in exchange and a prosperous time for banks are shown. Evil aspects or an eclipse will cause fluctuation and perturbation in the money market, run on banks, fall in prices of stocks and shares.

A Lunation in the fourth house with good aspects favours agricultural concerns and increases the value of such stocks and shares. Evil aspects or an eclipse will show the contrary.

A Lunation in the tenth with good aspects favours and improves Government revenues and also rise in price of Government securities. With evil aspects or an eclipse, the State finance suffers and a fall in revenue may be expected. Also a fall in the prices of securities and corresponding reactions in the money market are shown.

Eclipses in the earthy signs cause fluctuations and depressions in the commercial world, in trade and agricultural affairs.

TRANSITS

The movements of the planets and the luminaries have significant influence in the course of fluctuations of the values of stocks and shares and of commodities.

When a planet transits over the place of conjunction or opposition of a luminary in an Ingress figure, eclipse map, or in the map of the conjunction of any two superior planets, remarkable effects will happen according to the nature of the planet and of the house in which the transit occurs, and a corresponding reaction in the market is observed.

When the Sun comes to the place of conjunction, square or opposition of a malefic in such figures, unfavourable market with fall in values of stocks and shares is indicated, and the influence works from one to two days forward and similar number of days after the exact transit.

Such transits of the Moon are also important, but they work only for an hour or so.

The days on which both the luminaries form evil transits to malefics at the same time, will be more unfavourable than other days.

Good transits, such as conjunction to a benefic or to the place of a benefic aspect of any planet will generally bring good results.

CHAPTER XI

Charting the Value Curve

If the series of successive monthly, quarterly or any such adequate periodic values of stocks or commodities is shown over ten or twelve years and a line is drawn through these several figures, a rough curve would thus be produced, with many and curious twists and variations of outline, but in general, and broadly, it would be perceived that there is a point where the curve begins distinctly to ascend continuously (notwithstanding small intermediate irregularities in the progress), which indicates the time where the price is the lowest, and a point also whence it commences to descend definitely (with minor interposed breaks), which shows the time when the price is at its highest. If planetary configurations are similarly considered for these periods it will also be found that important evil aspects between them correspond with the lowest value points and that important good aspects between the planets correspond with the highest value points indicated above.

The calculation of the value curves is to be made for each country from its Mundane Quarterly Ingress maps, Lunation figures, transits therein and also the daily aspects formed between the planets. Generally the aspects formed by the transits of the planets in the quarterly and lunation figures and the mutual aspects formed between the planets themselves are considered. A good aspect indicates a rise, and an evil aspect, a fall in price.

In order to draw up a chart, one should note the daily aspects formed between the planets and also the transits in the quarterly and lunation figures for the particular required period, say during a lunar month commencing from a new moon or in relation to a calendar month.

Thus :

Transits in	Days of Month									
	1	2	3	4	5	6	7	8	9	&c.
Quarterly Figure										
Lunation Figure										
Daily Aspects										

Note the aspects for each group under the proper date and chart them in the graph as explained below.

In charting, the law of averages is one of the chief principles. From the highest price which a stock or a commodity may have reached during a term of years, subtract the lowest price which has been recorded for the same stock or commodity during the same period, adding to that half the difference, which may be taken as the *norm* of the stock or commodity. A survey of at least five years is a fair basis of calculation.

Draw a horizontal line representing this norm and divide this into as many equal sections as shall represent months over which your observations are required to extend. Subdivide these sections into periods of five or ten days each and against them put the day of the month thus indicated. Then make a graph which is six lines above and six below the norm line. This total of twelve lines yields a thirty-degrees angle for each. Plot the favourable conjunction and parallel to the top line of the graph, the 120-degrees aspect to the fourth line, the 60-degrees aspect to the second line above the norm line. Below it, the third line is the 90-degrees aspect, and the adverse conjunction or parallel, or opposition reaches the bottom line. Thus we obtain the provision for all of the major aspects, with possibility for including semi-squares, quintiles, sesqui-quadrates, etc.

Sort out the aspects formed during the required period consecutively and put them against the dates on which they are formed, placing the benefic aspects above the norm and the evil aspects below it, each exactly on the vertical sub-divisional line representing the date on which it is formed. Now take a pencil and starting from the earliest date draw a line upwards or downwards as the case may be, to the first of the aspects formed, proceeding upwards or downwards to the next aspect and so on, according to the nature of the aspects charted in the above manner. You will obtain a typical up-and-down continuous line crossing the norm at irregular intervals, which will indicate with great precision the rise and fall of the price.

When an aspect is exact note its mark on the proper place and then until its orb is expired, it will gradually decline. But if it continues within the orb and reaches again to its exact point, this change should be proportional. For example, suppose the orb is 8 degrees and the aspect moves at 4 degrees, therefore the change is noted slightly below than its exact position in the scale, and so on.

When several different kinds of items such as quarterly and lunation figures and the mutual aspects between the planets, are to be considered together, different signs for the graphs should be used and then a mean line of all these lines should be drawn, which will show the correct line of the value curve. For example, the daily aspects may be noted by – – – – . the transits in the lunation figure by ············, and those in the quarterly figure by – / – / – / – / – ; then finally a mean is struck from these and marked by a continuous line ————— ——.

As an example we take the case of Indian Iron and Steel, which was incorporated on the 11th March, 1918 at Calcutta. It is the pulse and barometer of the Calcutta Stock Exchange. The horoscope of the Company is given in page 79.

In this horoscope we find Gemini 28½ degrees rising and Mercury culminating in conjunction with the Sun ; Moon is in conjunction with Uranus in the 9th house and Jupiter is in sextile aspect with Saturn and Neptune and is in conjunction with Fortuna. All these show that the Company has a bright future.

From directions it is found that during 1935 and 1936 Saturn was in opposition to Uranus, and Neptune was in opposition to the Sun and Z. P., and Saturn transited the 10th house. This period was therefore bad for the prospect of the Company and actually no dividend was declared for these two years. For 1937 the directions were : Sun trine Saturn, Mars trine Venus, Fortuna trine Uranus. This year the Company made good profits and declared a dividend of 20%. The directions for 1938 were Saturn opposition Moon, Z. P. trine Saturn, Venus trine Saturn, Asc. trine Mercury. Venus square Jupiter, Moon conjunction Z. P. The major significators having good directional aspects, further prosperity was indicated, though there was some struggle due to a few evil directions, a dividend of 35% was declared for this year. In 1939 the evil direction of Jupiter square Mars brought the dividend down to 15 and again in 1940 the dividend rose to 20% due to the directions of the significators Fortuna conjunction Asc., Uranus conjunction Z P., Sun conjunction Moon. In 1941 and 1942 the directions Jupiter trine Moon, Uranus conjunction Mercury, and also the Sun, Jupiter conjunction Asc., brought a further rise in the dividend to $2\frac{1}{2}$% for each of these two years, particularly as Jupiter was transiting the Asc. during these two years, though Neptune opposition Moon hampered its progress slightly to obtain more profits. In 1943, Sun sextile

Venus, though a good direction, was hampered by the transit of Saturn over the Ascendant and the dividend fell to 20%.

As further illustration and graphical chart, we will now consider the daily fluctuation of the values of the Company in the market for the month of January, 1943. We should therefore first of all

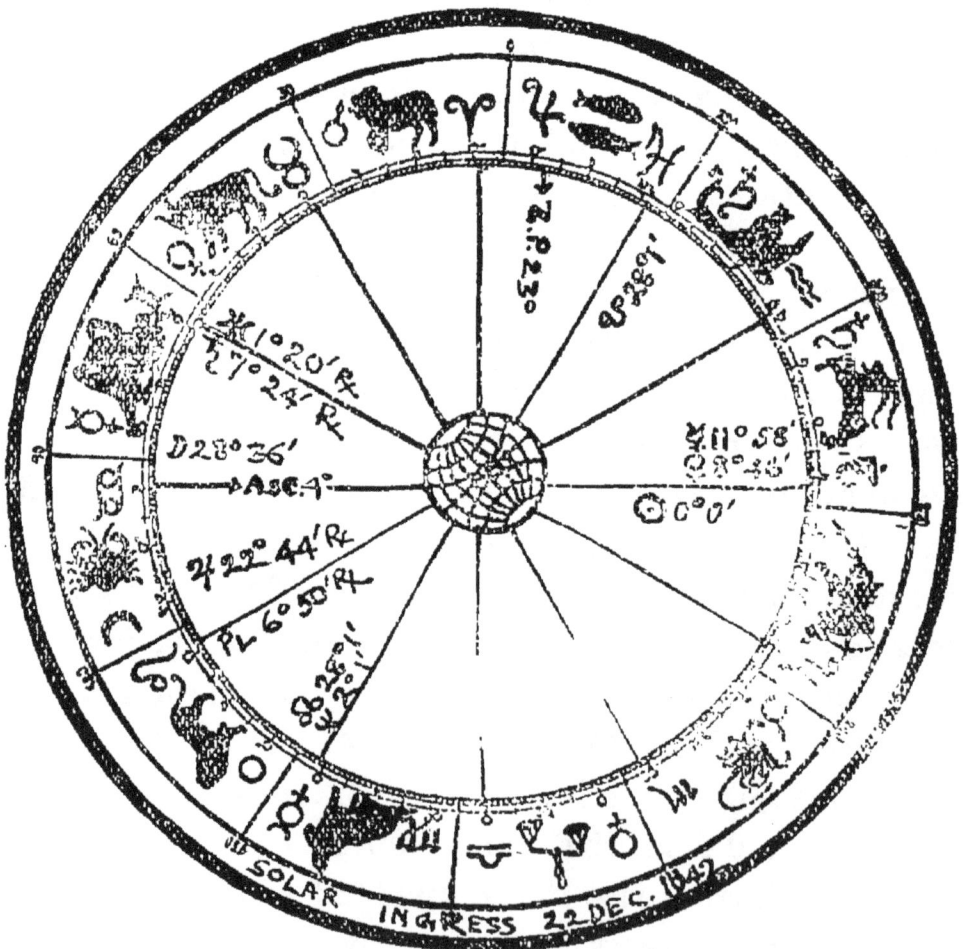

SOLAR INGRESS 22 DEC. 1942

consider the previous Ingress Map of 22nd December, 1942, 5. 34 p. m., Calcutta for the entry of the Sun into Capricorn and also the Lunation map in the month of January, which took place on the 6th January, 1943, 6. 33 p. m., Calcutta. As iron is ruled by Mars, the transits of Mars in these two maps are to be considered. As no transits over the important positions in the Lunation figure are found, we need not consider this map. The figure for the Ingress map is given above.

The following chart constructed according to the instructions given in the foregoing pages, will show the transits and daily aspects during January, 1943. In the graph the transits are shown by ·········. and the daily aspects of Mars are·shown by — — — —, and the actual price curve by ———. As there are no transits of Mars in the Lunation figure, they are not shown.

Transits of Mars in the Ingress Map	6. Merc. sextile Mars, 17. Mars sq. Z. P., 24. Mars opp. Moon, 27. Mars conj. Sun, 30. Mars sq. Neptune.
Lunation Map	Nil
Daily Aspects	1. Mercury par. Mars, 3. Venus par. Mars, 5. Sun par. Mars, 11. Venus semi-square Mars, 19. Mercury semi-sq. Mars, 29. Mars square Neptune. The principal major aspect between superior planets is Mars opp. Uranus.

JANUARY 1943

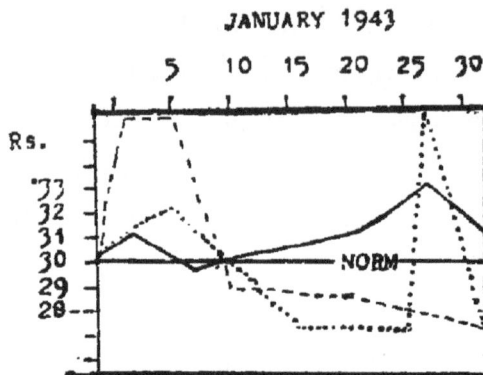

The period has the position of the North Node in Sagittarius, which indicates that the price of commodities will be on the rise during the coming years and actually the prices of all commodities and shares rose considerably during 1944 to 1946. But the prevailing aspect of the major planets Mars oppositon Uranus in this particular period shows a temporary depression in the share market.

During the 1st and the 5th of this month the price rose due to the parallel aspects and favourable transit. From the 5th to the 17th the price fell due to the evil aspects and transit. Form the 21st the price rose up to the 27th due to Sun conjunction Mars, but declined from 29th due to evil aspect and transit of Mars.

When the general price fluctuations in the share market are to be considered the transits and aspects of all the planets are to be considered together in the manner similar to the above.

CHAPTER XII

Planetary Influence on Stock Exchange

The trend of stock market prices tends to conform to the major trends of the Market. But still it is under a set of individual conditions of its own. These governing planetary factors may be ascertained by studying the chart of the Stock Exchange of the locality concerned.

Certain markets have a group influence and may be considered together. These have joint indicators indicated by the ruler of the particular house of the Stock Exchange Chart. For example, when the Railroad Shares are to be considered the third house of the chart is to be judged. Also the Stock Exchange Map itself will indicate the trend of the markets which are the principal features of the place. For example, the Cotton spinning and weaving industries are for Bombay ; Jute, Tea, Coal, etc., for Calcutta ; Copra, Coffee, Groundnut, etc., for Madras. Similarly, for other places of the world. The special house indications of a Stock Exchange Map are the same as described in chapter IX.

The vital points of a Stock Exchange Horoscope are the Zenith and Nadir points, the points occupied by the Ascendant and Descendant, the points occupied by the Sun and the Moon and their opposite points, and also the planet which rules the sign occupied by the Sun is important. The Part of Fortune is also considered as important. These are called the Significators.

Planets transiting the angles of the Stock Exchange Map show the market conditions, and aspects of the ruler of the tenth house by the major planets will indicate the trend of market prices. Also we must look to the transits of the major planets over the Significators for the big movements and to the ephemeral aspects to the planet ruling the sign occupied by the Sun for the fluctuations.

A major planet passing over the Zenith Point of the Stock Exchange Map indicates the future as long as the planet transits the meridian. Any benefic planet or the Moon's North Node which passes through the meridian, indicates an advance in price, but if the planet is a malefic one, a financial panic or business crisis is indicated.

The monthly trends of the market are indicated from the planetary positions falling in the Stock Exchange Map at lunations. The good or evil aspects of the lunation planets with the chart significators will indicate the trend for advance or fall. If the Lunation indicates a change in the trend for the ensuing month, watch for the days when the Moon passes through the cardinal signs. The change will usually occur on one of these days. If the Lunation falls in conjunction, sextile, square, trine or opposition to a planet in the tenth house, the market will react according to the indication of the aspect when the Moon passes over that important point in the following month.

The positions of the planets in the Lunation are to be placed in their proper places in the Stock Exchange Chart and observe :

(1) If any of the major planets falls in the tenth house ; if any planet falls either in the first, fourth or

in the seventh house of the chart. Aspects to these
planets at the lunation are highly important in making
market forecasts. Planets on the mid-heaven are the
most important of all in making judgment of the trend
of the market. These planets are to be taken into
account along with the ruler of the tenth house of the
Stock Exchange Chart.

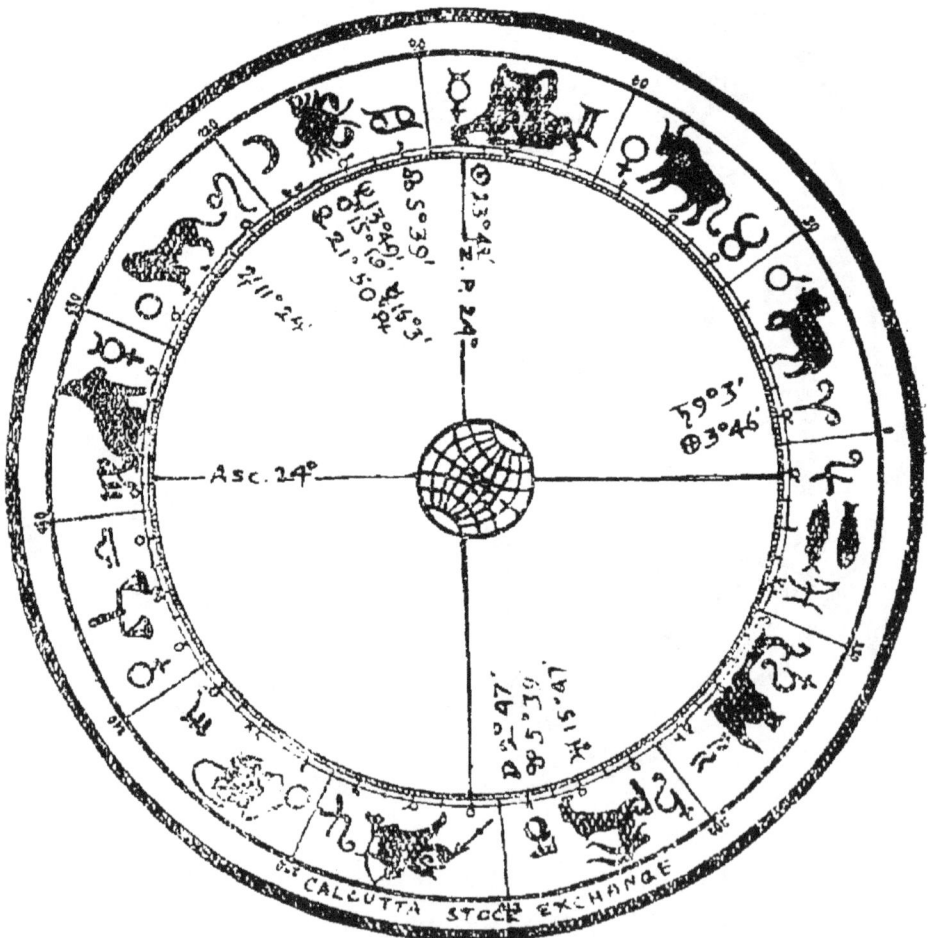

(2) If the Lunation receives a favourable or
unfavourable aspect from the ruler of the tenth house,

and also it receives a favourable or unfavourable aspect from the planet accidentally found in the tenth house.

(3)   Whether Saturn and Uranus are in favourable or unfavourable aspect or not in any aspect at all. A favourable aspect between them indicate a rise, and an unfavourable aspect, a fall in price.   If the conjunction of Saturn and Uranus is powerfully aspected by

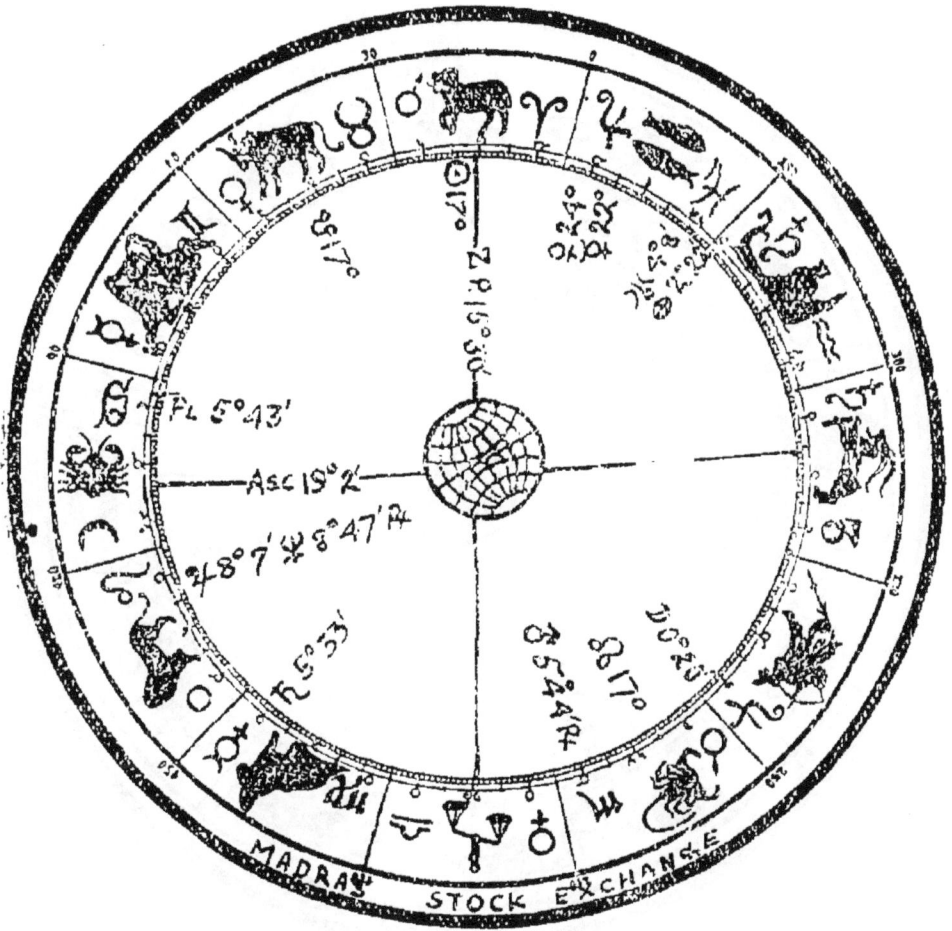

MADRAS STOCK EXCHANGE

Jupiter from an angle house, there may or may not be a drop in prices.

It is a noticeable fact that when there is a sharp

drop or sharp rise in the stock market, the Moon is usually found in one of the angular houses of the Stock Exchange Chart.

These indications will show the large variety and range of the affairs which may enter into the business of a Stock Exchange and find reflection in the horoscope of that institution. The lunation, ingress, con-

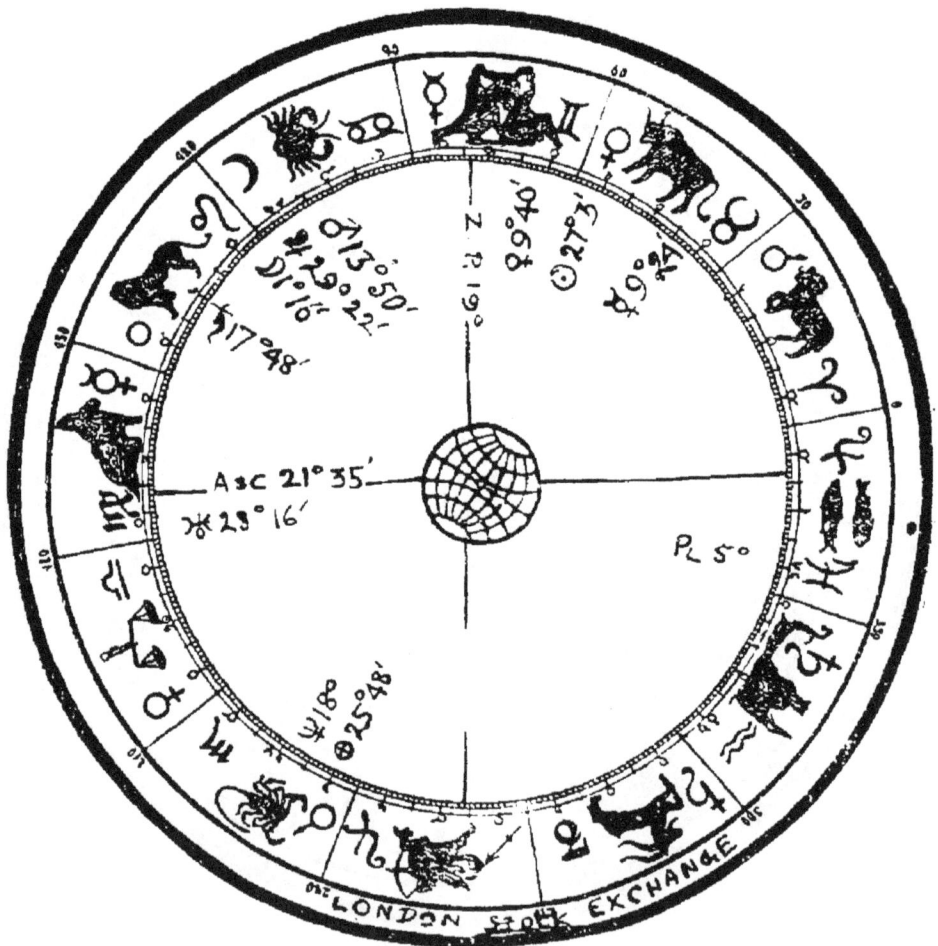

junction of the major planets, eclipse, etc., all have significance when falling in the several houses of this horoscope.

The Bombay Stock Exchange Chart is for 4 p.m.,
8th January, 1899 ; Calcutta Stock Exchange Chart is
or noon, 15th June, 1908 ; Madras Stock Exchange,
ioon, 7th April, 1920. The British Stock Exchange was
nstituted at London on the 18th May, 1801 at 1. 30
).m., and the American Stock Exchange at New York
)n the 18th May, 1792, noon. It is said to be organized

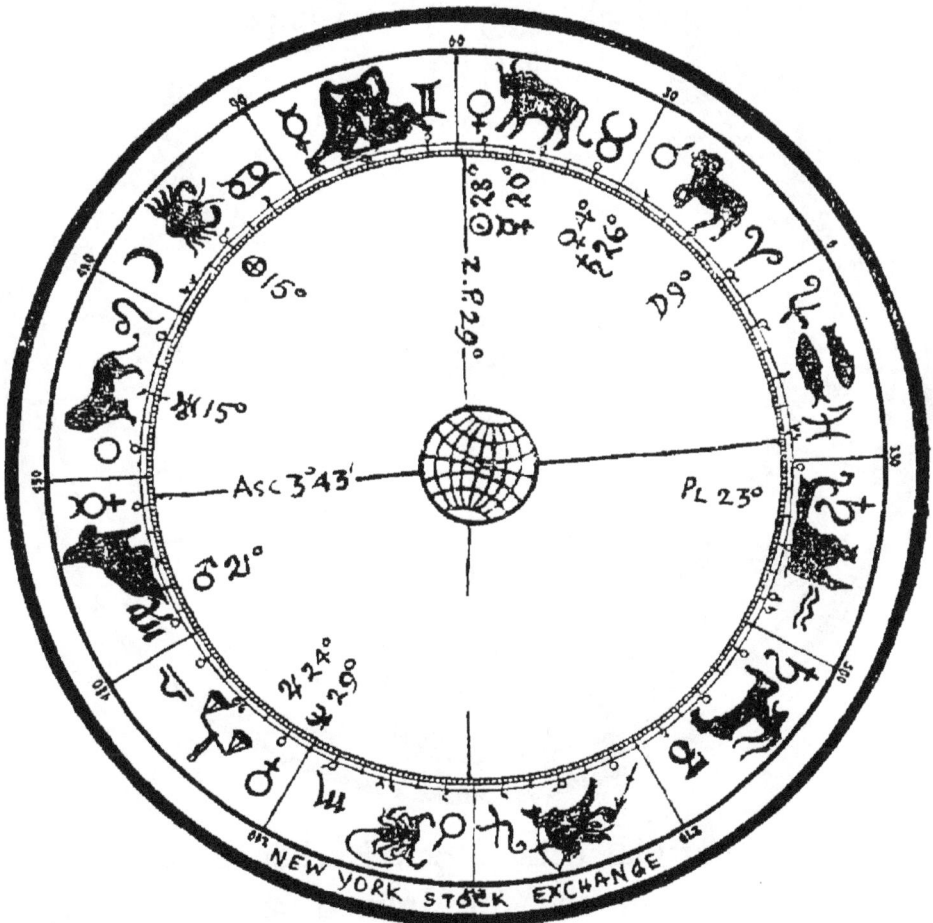

it 11. 7 a.m. of the 17th May. The map for the 18th
Vlay, however, is considered in all judgments of the
narket. The New York Stock Exchange was again

reorganized at 11. 20 a.m. on the 22nd April, 1903. Some take Pisces 24 to 28 degrees on the meridian and Cancer 14 to 17 degrees on the Ascendant of this New York Stock Exchange.

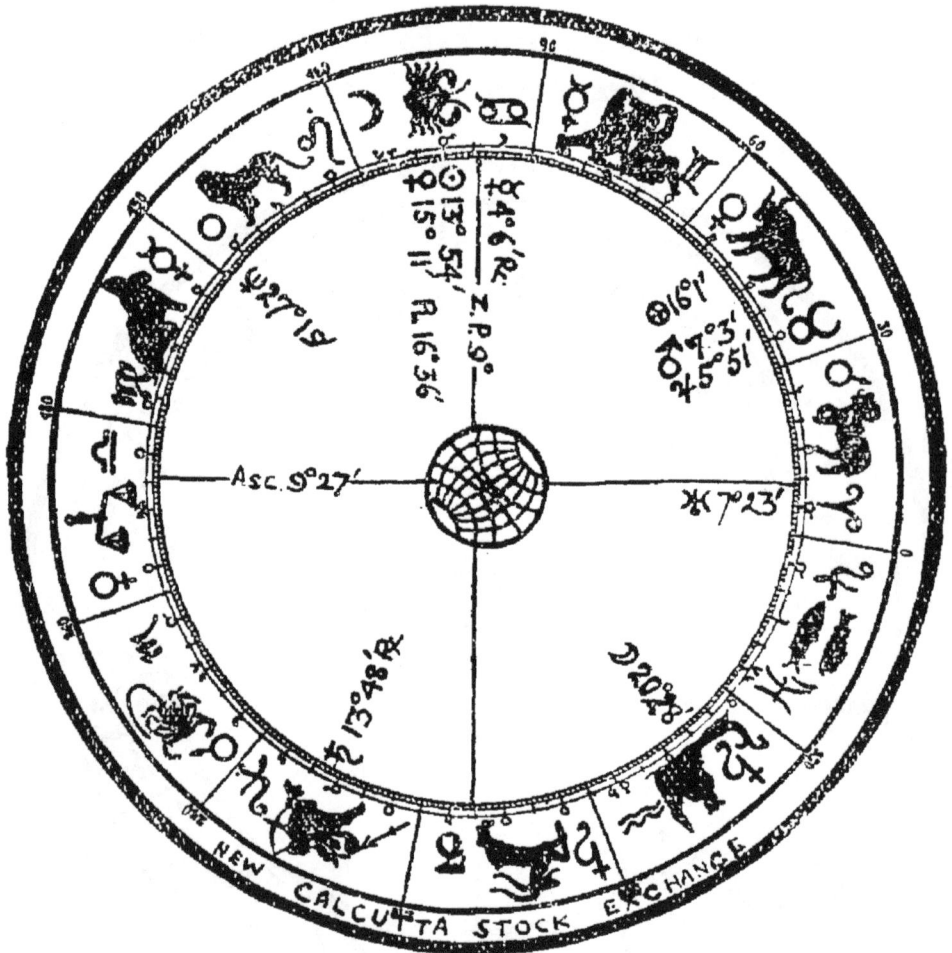

The present Calcutta Stock Exchange was opened at 11. 45 a.m. on the 6th July, 1928. The Calcutta Jute Exchange was founded at 5 p.m. on the 14th September, 1936.

There is also another horoscope of Bombay Stock Exchange for the 9th July, 1875 at 11. 22 a.m. local

time for Bombay. The figure is given below. Here
the Zenth Point is at 7° Cancer and the Ascendant at
7° 12′ Libra. The transits and aspects of the planets
to these points have been found highly significant.

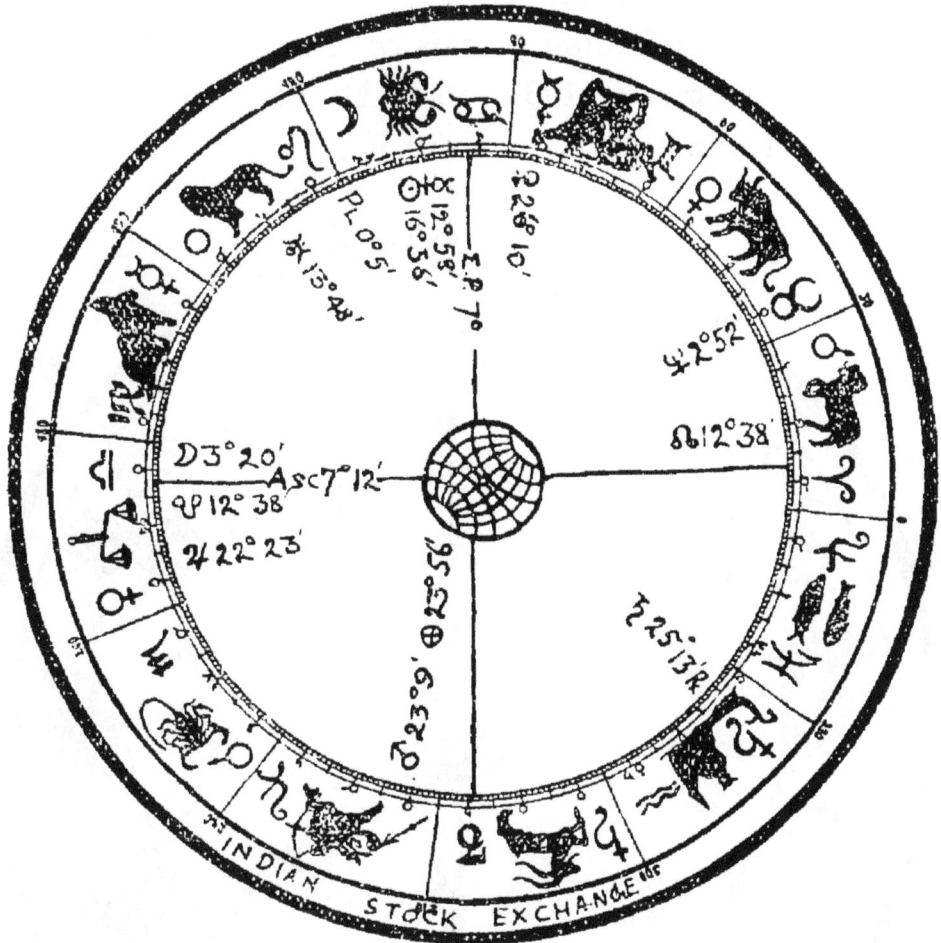

During 1930 Jupiter was in opposition to Saturn about
the Zenth Point, great political disturbances happened
in India and civil disobediance campaign was launched
and the Indian Stock Market recorded a marked fall,
until in 1933 by the transit of Jupiter over the ascendant the market recovered and showed a colossal

inflation in most of the well known share values. Similar events happened in 1945-46, when Jupiter and Neptune transited the ascendant, while from August 1946, there was a grest slump in the market due to the transits of Mars and Neptune over the ascendant.

A new Stock Exchange was registered in Bombay on the 5th November, 1937 and the map for this may also be cast and studied with profit.

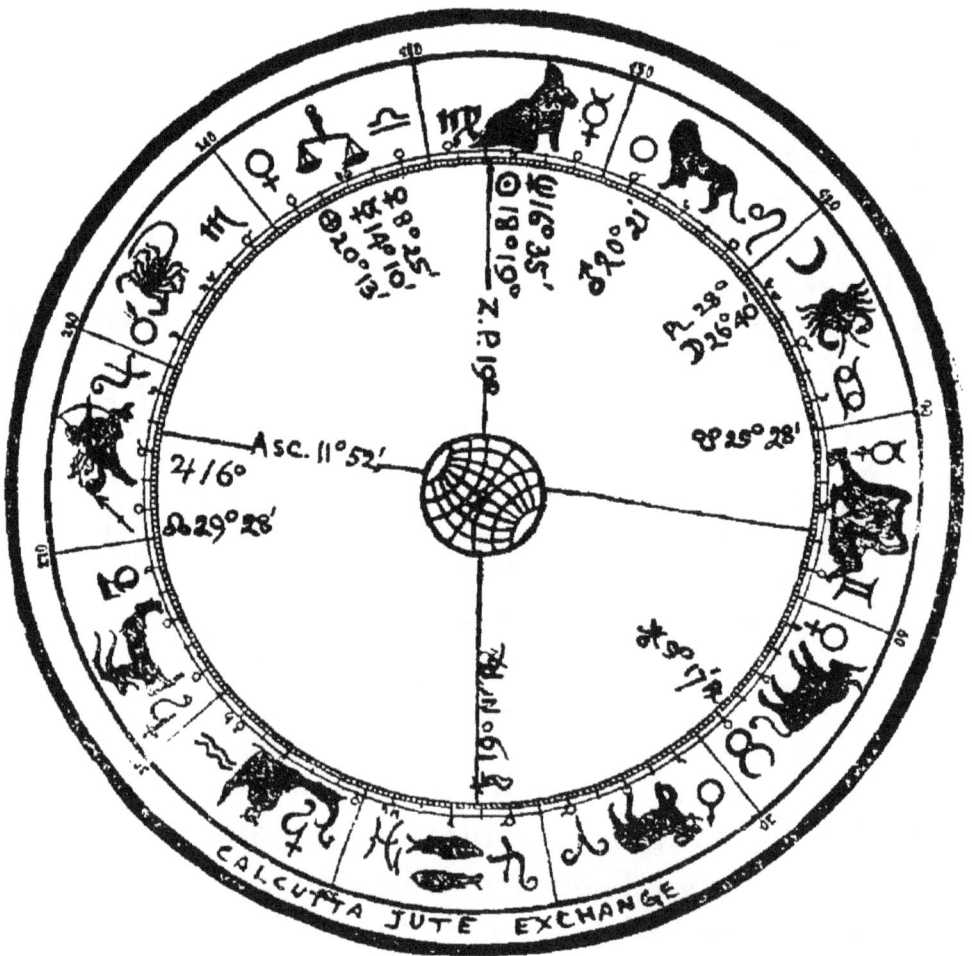

CHAPTER XIII

Planetary Cycles and Mundane Events

Like the Solar Ingress at the Vernal Equinox and Lunations, there are Planetary Cycles for each planet, which also show the general mundane events and the trend of the market condition. Similar to the change of the Sun of its declination at the vernal equinox, the moment when a planet changes from South declination to North declination, that is, when it reaches $0°$ N. Decl., is considered as the commencement of the cycle of influence of that planet in mundane affairs, and a horoscope erected at any particular place for this moment indicates by the position and aspects of this particular planet, the influence on the things related to or ruled by this planet during its ensuing cycle concerning such affairs for the locality. This horoscope continues to be effective until the commencement of the next Cycle of the same planet, and reveals the events that will transpire due to the influence of the activities ruled by the planet for which it is erected. The Sun's Ingress Chart for the vernal equinox and the charts for lunations indicate the influence on all kinds of affairs of the locality for which erected, but the Cycle charts of other planets only confine to definite affairs and commodites ruled by the concerned planets and not to other unrelated affairs.

The events signified by a Cycle Chart may begin to happen somewhat before the Cycle actually starts, for the planet begins to exert its influence when it is within one degree of crossing the equator and continues to exert the influence during the time it is within one degree after crossing. In a Cycle Chart the only planet that is directed to form aspects with other planets is the planet for which the Chart is erected and the time of events is derived from the daily transits to the aspects and positions of the other planets and sensitive points. Thus, the mundane affairs, the fluctuations in price of commodites, stocks, etc., ruled by the planet, which have already been described in the previous chapters, can be ascertained form the transits and aspects to the Zenith Point, Ascendant and other planets of this horoscope, and the dates of events are indicated by the dates of transits, etc.

The Cycles of the major planets, Pluto, Neptune, Uranus, Saturn, Jupiter and Mars are important and are therefore used for forecasts of both mundane events and market conditions, as their durations are long, while those of Venus and Mercury are not considered as important for mundane affairs, but is used for short time market conditions, as they are of short duration.

In politics, Pluto is said to rule groups, co-operation, the spilling into two opposite factors, and the exercise of dictatorial powers. Nepture rules visionary schemes, involved affairs, secret plots, etc. ; Uranus rules revolution, reforms, strikes, exposure, invention, etc. ; Saturn represents economy, poverty, basic utilities, buildings, crops, mines, labour, destruction, etc. ; Jupiter rules finance, trade, treaties, arbitration, public expression of opinion, religion, etc. ; Mars governs war, army, police, magistrates, doctors, industrial workers, fires, vice, gambling, robbery, accidents, strife, etc.

Thus, for example, the Mars Cycle commences on the 6th May, 1945 at 8h. 10m. 13s. a.m., Calcutta local time. The horoscope shows 15° Pisces culminating and 27° Gemini rising. The Sun was at 15° Taurus, Mercury 20° Aries, Venus 17° Aries retrograde, Mars at 2°31' Aries, Moon at 26° Aquarius, Jupiter $17\frac{1}{2}°$ Virgo retrograde, Saturn 7° Cancer, Uranus $11\frac{1}{2}°$ Gemini and Neptune 4° Libra retrograde. Mars in this horoscope shows to be strongly posited in the tenth house in sextile aspect to Uranus, but square to Saturn and opposition to Neptune. This shows that the Iron Shares will open with a lower price tendency but will make a considerable rise gradually. From the 17th to 28th May, Mars transited the places of Venus and Mercury and also the sextile aspect of Uranus, the market rose form Rs. 39 to Rs. 40. On the 21st June, Mars transited the sextile of Saturn, the price rose to Rs. 41/7. From the 2nd to 5th July, Mars transited the trine aspect of

Jupiter and the price rose up to Rs. 42. From the 9th to 15th August, Mars transited Uranus and the square aspect of the Zenith Point of the horoscope, the price fell to Rs 39. On the 3rd September, Mars transited over the Ascendant and the price rose up to Rs. 41/5, but from the 15th to 20th it transited the square aspect of Neptune and over the place of Saturn and the price fell to Rs. 41. Again, on the 9th October, it transited the square aspects of Venus and Mercury and the sextile aspect of Jupiter retrograde, the latter being weak, and also the trine of the Zenith Point, the price remained practically steady at about Rs. 41. From the 21st November to 17th December, Mars came to the trine of Mars in the horoscope and was coming to the sextile aspect of Uranus, the price gradually rose up to Rs. 56.

Another example : a Cycle of Mars commenced at Calcutta on the 15th April, 1947 at 4h. 0m. 19s. a. m., when Pisces 20° was rising and Sagittarius 23° was culminating ; the Sun was at 24° Aries, Moon 10° Aquarius, Mercury 28° Pisces, Venus 17½° Pisces, Mars 2° Aries, Jupiter 26° Virgo retrograde, Saturn 2° Leo, Uranus 19° Gemini, Neptune 9° Libra retrograde, and Pluto 11° Leo retrograde. In this Cycle Chart Mars was in opposition to Neptune, trine to Saturn and in conjunction with Mercury. The Stocks on Iron shares showed a general trend of fall in price due to some mysterious causes as indicated by the opposition of Neptune and also Uranus opposition to the Zenith Point of this horoscope.

In the beginning of August, Mars came to the opposition of the Zenith Point and there was a fall in the price of Iron stocks ; on the 14th November, Mars came to the trine of the Z. P., but as about this time and also from November, 1947 Uranus came to the exact opposition of the Z. P., the rise indicated by the trine of Mars was very slight and, on the other hand, there was a strong trend towards a fall ; and as the transit of Uranus lasts over a long period, the depression continued for a long time. In 1948 February, Jupiter transited over the Z. P. and towards the end of February and beginning of March, Mars came to the trine of Z. P., and also in the beginning of May when Mars again came to the trine of Z. P., there was a temporary rise in price. In July Mars came to the square of both Uranus and Z. P. and there was a heavy fall in price, from which it will take a long time to make a recovery of the market due to the influence of Uranus.

It must, however, be noted that only Cycle Charts do not solely indicate the trend of the market. All the other factors are also to be considered together.

In order to follow the trend of the market from day to day make a chart according to the following table and note from the Ephemeris the daily transits formed and aspects by the planets and luminaries and also the directional aspects to the radical positions in the Ingress, Lunation, Stock Exchange, Planetary Cycles and other Charts.

CHART

Dates of the Month

1   2   3   4   5   &c.

1. Daily Aspects
2. Solar Ingress
3. Lunation
4. Conjunction of Major Planets
5. Planetary Cycles
6. Stock Exchange Horoscope
7. Political Chart of a Country

The first five terms are useful for the entire world, but the house positions will vary. On reading your daily paper about the various events, either on political, mundane or market, or on weather conditions, refer to the aspects near about the day in reference to the radical Charts used and you will find the indications to correspond with the events.

This mode of application of the transits should be used in all kinds of market forecasting.

CHAPTER XIV

Individual Corporation

If you are an investor it is usually important that you should be able to discover the condition of, let us say, some corporation whose shares you are tempted to purchase. The prospects of a Corporation can be easily judged from its horoscope and future directions just as can be done in the case of the nativity of an individual person.

For the horoscope of a Corporation take the date on which it was incorporated or registered and erect the horoscope in the usual manner for noon of that date. Some astrologers consider the moment of signing the papers of the Corporation by the directors, as shall govern its future activities, as the proper time of its horoscope. But generally the former horoscope proves to be quite satisfactory. You can calculate the directions in the chart just as with a natal figure by progressing all the factors of the horoscope and the planets at the rate of 1 degree for every year from the date of incorporation and also by taking the transits of the major planets over the significators of the horoscope into consideration. The indications are to be taken in conformity with those of the general aspects between the major planets and from the current Ingress and Lunation figures.

You proceed by studying the Ingress figure to see the present state of affairs in respect of such articles as interest the Corporation. Then you consider the Lunation figure and the general aspects between the major planets to see how the present month affects such commodities. Ascertaining the general trend of the market, you can then examine the chart of the particular corporation and from its directional indications make your decision.

As stated above the horoscope of a corporation is to be cast for noon of the day of its registration or incorporation. After the horoscope is cast, the positions of the Sun, Moon and the planets and also the place of the Part of Fortune should be properly inserted in the figure. The Part of Fortune is calculated by adding the sign, degrees, minutes of the longitude of the Moon to that of the Ascendant and subtracting from the total the longitude of the Sun. The Zenith Point, Ascendant, Sun, Moon and the Part of Fortune are called the Significators of the horoscope.

The significations of the houses of the horoscope have been fully described in a previous chapter, but here we are dealing exclusively with those principal houses that have a bearing on the stock and share market. These are the angle houses of the horoscope ; the first represents the public ; the tenth, the Government, the managing body or the directors ; the seventh, the opponent or rival companies, war condition, Government or executive policies affecting the business and stock market; and the fourth, the property, products, growing crops, mines, oil, coal, and all that comes from the weather condition.

In studying the chart of a Corporation, one other planetary factor is to be carefully considered and that is called the Indicator. This is the planet which rules the sign in which the Sun is posited on the date of registration of the Company. Thus, the Sun in Aries gives Mars as the Indicator, the Sun in Taurus gives Venus as the Indicator, and so on. The aspects of the Indicator will also show the prospects of the Company.

The first step after erecting the horoscope, is to study the planetary positions and aspects in the figure, particularly of the Sun, Moon and Jupiter. These give the indications of the life, public relationship and financial possibilities of the Company. A retrograde planet has no strong influence in the chart.

The Sun represents the organization, management, aims and products of the Company. His aspects and directions therefore show the possibilities of profit and loss of the Company.

The Moon represents the buying public. Her favourable or unfavourable aspects show the attitude of the people towards the Company. If badly aspected, the Company has to work under a heavy handicap and even has to go out of business sooner or later.

Mars indicates the strength and activity of the stock on the market. His evil aspect to Jupiter is unfavourable.

Jupiter represents the money making possibilities of the Company, and Saturn represents the set-backs and financial difficulties which the Company is apt to experience. His unfavourable aspects to the luminaries indicate many financial vicissitudes of the Company. The other planets influence favourably or unfavourably according to their aspects to the luminaries and the Indicator.

The fortunate or unfortunate periods of the Company are ascertained by progressing the Significators as well as the planets by adding 1 degree for 1 year from the date of registration of the Company and then noting the conjunction and aspects formed by the Significators to the radical planets and also by the planets to the radical positions of the Significators. The conjunction of Venus and Jupiter, and also of the Sun, Moon and Mercury, when themselves well aspected in the horoscope, and also the benefic aspects of all planets are good and show a rise in share value and profit of the Company. The conjunction of Neptune, Uranus, Saturn or Mars and the evil aspects of all planets are bad and bring a fall in the value and indicate loss and a difficult period of the Company.

The function of the Indicator is to determine the course of fluctuation of the value of the stock from the daily aspects it receives from the planets, showing the trend of the share value of the Company from day to day.

The transits of the major planets, Neptune, Uranus, Saturn, Jupiter and Mars over the places and aspects of the radical Significators and also over their directional positions are to be considered from the current Ephemeris ; also the aspects of the planets to the Indicator are to be noted. The former have the greater influence and the latter a secondary influence. A transit may last for several days while an aspect to the Indicator does not last more than a day. The influence of the directions is of first importance, then the transits of the major planets over the Significators, and lastly the ephemeral aspects formed to the Indicator. But all these are subject to the general trend shown by the aspects between the major planets themselves, by the Ingress and Lunation figures and eclipses, etc. Indications taken according to this principle will lead to a correct judgment.

The transit of Mercury or its aspect to the Indicator is important since it always act in terms of the planet to which it was last in aspect within three days, and the nature of that aspect will determine whether its transit is good or bad. But if it is not in any aspect during the preceding three days, then see what sign it is in and consider it to be of the nature of the ruler of that sign. Its good aspect shows activity and rise in price, and its evil aspect, a fall.

Venus by good aspects enhances the share values, but by evil aspects shows a stagnant market.

Mars often stimulates the market and always does so by his good aspects, but his evil aspects cause panicky effects due to disputes or war possibilities. He is always involved when there is an active stock market either for buying or selling.

Jupiter gives a rise by his conjunction or good aspects, but his evil aspects show selling for profit-taking.

Whenever Saturn transits the Significators in an unfavourable way, it is usually a bad year for the Company. Saturn affects by misfortune of some kind. His good aspects steady the market but do not much inflate it. His conjunction or evil aspects never fail to depress it.

The effects of Uranus are sudden and not sustained ; they are by strikes and dissensions. He shows quick turn of the market. His evil aspects affect the values through trade dislocations and strikes.

If the planets Uranus and Saturn are in benefic aspect to each other at the time of a favourable transit over the Significators, particularly the Sun or the Moon, the price will rise. But if they are in mutual evil aspect and at the same time unfavourably transit the Significators, the trend will be decidedly downward. Also when the major planets aspect the important planetary positions in the chart of a Company, there will be a big up or down movement in the value of the shares of the Company according to the nature of the aspect.

Neptune affects by revolutions, lapses and defections ; it shows cliques and groups acting together to engineer or rig the market, in good aspect to inflate values, and in evil aspect, to depress them.

The transits over the radical Significators coinciding with an ephemeral aspect to the Indicator of the same kind, will produce a sudden effect. The effects of the transits generaly last for several days and weeks.

Eclipses falling on the places of the Significators are also to be considered and they are generally detrimental to the share values of the Company due to causes judged from the house in which the eclipses fall. On the date when a malefic planet makes the next transit over the place of the eclipse or its opposite, the effects will come into operation. The effects of eclipses last for a long time. The duration of the effects of a solar eclipse is the number of years three times of the digits eclipsed, and that of the lunar eclipse is the number of months seven times of the digits eclipsed. The transits of the malefic planets during these periods will cause many troubles. If the eclipse falls on the Meridian, the credit of the Company is affected; if on the Ascendant, the trouble will come through the personnel of the Company ; if on the Sun, through the director ; and if on the Moon, through public events ; also if on the Part of Fortune, the estate and the property of the Company will be affected.

A *boom* or abnormal rise in prices is indicated by a succession of good aspects to the Indicator and Significators without any intervening bad aspects from any planet. A *slump* is indicated conversely by a succession of evil aspects without interposing good aspects. A *choppy* market is indicated by a rapid succession of good and evil aspects.

For the consideration of the trend of the fluctuation

of values of an individual stock, we should therefore proceed in the following manner :

First of all, the aspects between the major planets and also the stationary position of Mars, when occurring, should be noted. These planetary configurations indicate the main trend of the stock market, and when two or more of these configurations of a similar nature (harmonious or inharmonious) operate at the same time, with no contradictory aspects, the indications according to the nature of the configurations are almost certain of fulfilment. But when the configurations are of opposite import (one harmonious and the other inharmonious), the outlook is more or less uncertain, generally leading to the one having precedence over the other and by the indications of the Ingress figures and of the configurations between the minor planets. These configurations give us a picture of the principal trend of the market, operating sometimes when applying, becoming exact, or seperating, with varying effects according to the configurations of the minor planets.

Next, the secondary reactions are determined from the quarterly Ingress figures and the monthly fluctuations from the lunation figures and daily ephemeral aspects between the minor planets.

Finally, the directional aspects, transits and eclipses in the horoscope of the individual stock should be considered in combination with the above indications. At various times a transiting planet is found to be retrograde, stationary and again becomes direct in movement. At these times it has most potent effect, especially, if it happens to be in close aspect to another planet at the same time.

For investment purpose the stocks or shares should not be chosen in whose horoscope the malefic planets occupy the places of the luminaries or the ascendant.

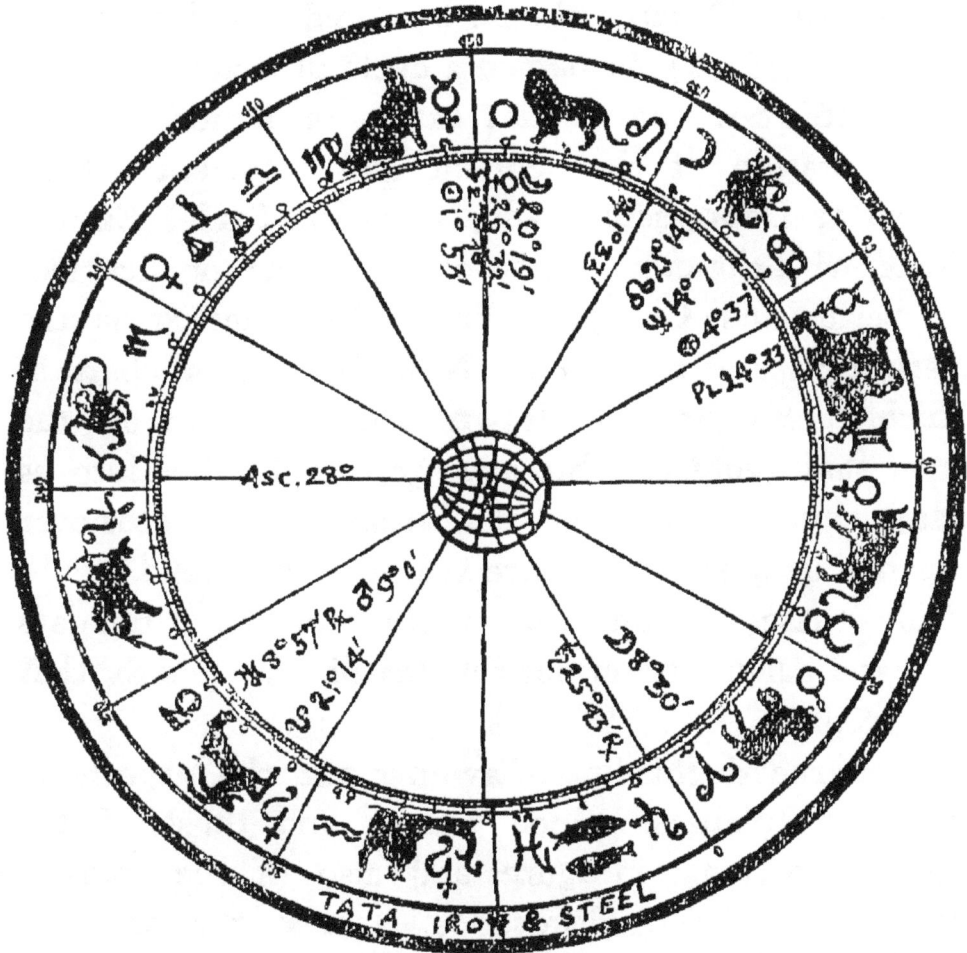

But for speculation purpose stocks and shares should be so chosen that none is intimately and mainly dependant upon one another, for, if the money be confined, exclusively or largely to one kind only, there will be the risk of depreciation or loss in all the holdings at one and the same time.

"Buy before a rise in value and sell before a fall" is a golden rule which has an admirable sound, but it is futile unless it is capable of being embodied in some practical workable shape. Therefore the prices for a term of 10 or 11 years should be noted, for looking to the course of what is named a cycle in commerce and trade ; this term allows that extent of period for the representation of the sequent and recurrent effects known as Depressed Trade, Healthy Trade, Excited Trade, with the culmination of a Bubble or fictitious prosperity and Collapse. From these determine the average price of the Stock. Now lay out a chart in which a straight line drawn horizontally across the paper shall represent this average, divide this into as many equal sections as shall represent months over which your observations are required to extend. Subdivide these sections into periods of five or ten days each and against them put the day of the month thus indicated.

Underneath this line of average put the aspects of the major planets, minor planets and those of the Ingress and Lunation figures and also of the transits, etc., in the Stock Horoscope, against the dates on which they are formed. The good aspects will indicate a rise and evil aspects, a fall. All these have already been explained in the previous chapters. The transition points between the aspects of contrary nature should also be noted. Now take a pencil and starting

from the earliest date draw a line upwards or downwards according to the nature of the aspects to the
first of the aspects formed or to the transition point,
as the case may be, proceeding upwards or downwards
to the next aspect and so on. You will then have a

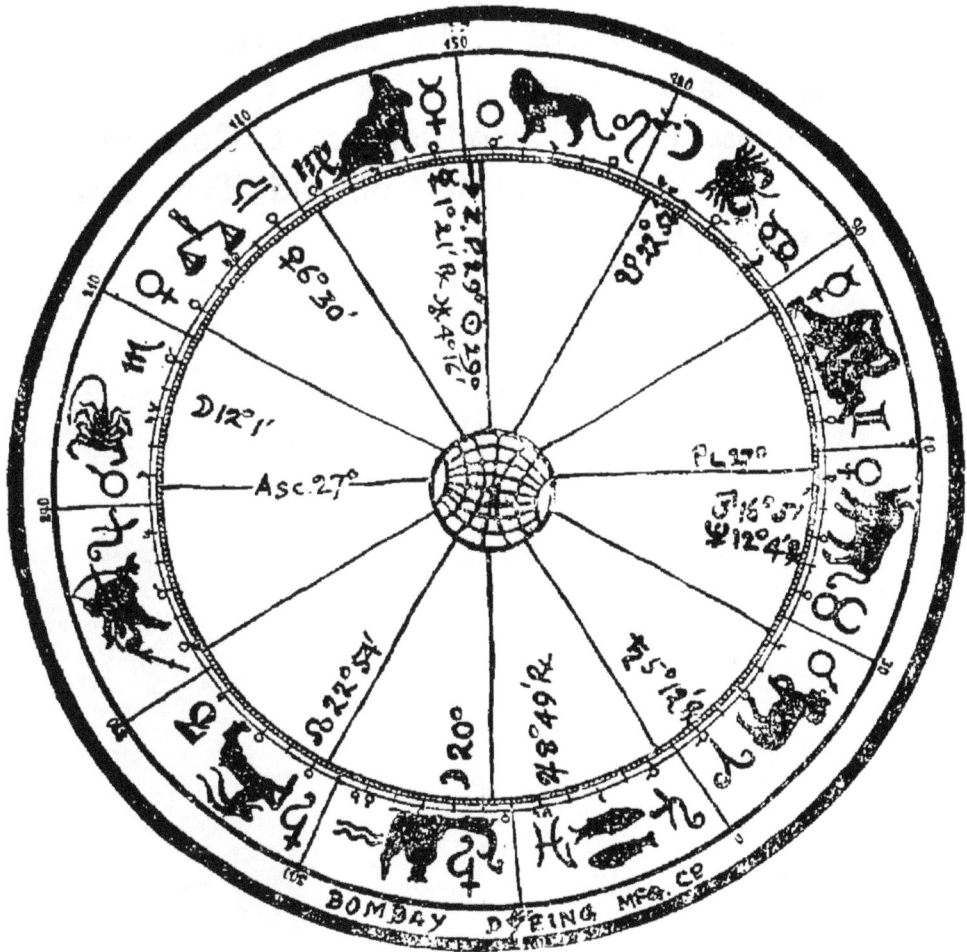

zigzag line crossing the line of average at irregular
intervals. When the line passes upwards the average
line, the time for thinking of selling will arrive,
while when it falls below the average line, a purchase

should be contemplated. Thus we shall be able to determine the trend of an individual stock value.

As a general rule for investment, avoid those stocks in which the evil planets on the day of incorporation occupied the place of the luminaries or the ascendant. The stocks in the horoscope of which benefic planets are close to the position of the luminaries or ascendant, are fortunate to trade in.

The horoscopes of two important Corporations, Bombay Dyeing Manufacturing Co., and Tata Iron & Steel, are given above.

CHAPTER XV

Produce Market

The concurrence of cyclical effects is produced upon the earth with a cyclically occurring condition of the Sun. The visible surface or disc of the Sun is intensely lustrous. At regularly recurrent intervals the uniform level of this intensely brilliant and enveloping surface is partially rent by cyclonic storms, possibly of an electric nature, into cavities or hollows which have received the name of spots. The area of spots, attaining a maximum, when the spots are abundant and extensive, and gradually declining to a minimum, when the spots are absent, proceeds in regulated rhythms of maximum and minimum of intervals of about 10 and 12 years. As the earth is traversed by magnetic currents, directly dependent upon the heat derived from the Sun, its material condition, its agricultural fertility or barrenness, its droughts and consequent famines, and the luxuriance or failure of crops, are associated with the state of its atmosphere as affected by the magnetic currents from these Sun spots in a periodic manner corresponding to the 10 to 12 years between a solar maximum and minimum of spots.

Most of the agricultural and natural products of the earth have therefore a major period of 10 years and another of 12 years in succession. At these times the prices are generally high ; and also there is another period of 11 and 12 years alternately when the prices of the commodities are low. These cycles are therefore of use in determining the trend of the future market when used in connection with planetary indications. These cycles for any particular commodity can be easily determined from its past price records.

Crop conditions and business in general are indicated by the aspects of the planets that are formed as the Sun enters the cardinal signs in each year. The seasonal map during which the particular kinds of crops are produced will show the condition of these crops for the period. The crop condition of the particular produce is therefore to be considered from these ingress maps. The map for the locality which controls the particular produce market or where the crops are produced in abundance is generally considered. The method of calculation of the ingress maps and of judgment of the crop conditions has already been explained in a previous chapter.

From the judgment of the ingress maps it will be evident that much depends on the general weather condition of the locality as indicated by the planetary configurations and the student would do well to study the influence of the configurations of the planets on weather conditions as explained in our "Weather Forecasting" in which the periodic fluctuations of the Sun-spots have also been explained.

Certain parts of the world control the produce and prices of certain products, and any events happening in these parts would affect the crop and price conditions of the produce confined in these areas. The planets transiting the zodiacal signs ruling these parts will affect the crop conditions of the locality.

Thus, the great Cotton belt lies across the southern States of America and rules the world market. Hence a horoscope of this locality will indicate the crop condition.

The principal produces and commodities ruled by different places are as follows :

WHEAT—United States of America, Argentina, Russia, India.

SUGAR—India, Java, Cochin China, Malaya.

RICE—China, India, Burma.

TEA—India, China, Ceylon.

COTTON—United States, India.

IRON, STEEL—United States, Germany.

COAL—United States, United Kingdom.

PETROLEUM—Russia, United States.

WOOL—Australia, Argentina.

RUBBER—West Coast of Africa, East Indies.

COPPER—United States.

TIN—Malaya States.

GOLD—Transvaal, Australia, United States.

SILVER—Mexico.

SILK—China, Italy, Japan.

In India the following articles are the chief products of the places mentioned against them :

Butter and Ghee	... Aligarh.
Tobacco	... Arakan, Bengal, Bombay, Madras, Bihar, Orissa, U.P., Punjab, C.P., Berar, Assam.
Petroleum	... Menangyaumg (Burma).
Rubber	... Travancore, Madras, Coorg.
Coal	... Ranigunj, Jheria.
Wood, Timber	... Rangoon, Burma.
Rice : Winter—April to August (sowing)— Nov. to Jan. (harvesting). Autumn—April to July (sowing)— Aug. to Dec. (harvesting).	... Bengal, Madras, Burma.
Jute : March to May (sowing) July to Sept. (harvesting).	Dacca, N.rainganj, Bengal, Bihar, Orissa, Assam.
Gold	... Kolar.
Iron	... Jamshedpur, Asansol.
Cotton : March to Aug. (sowing)—Sept. to April (harvesting).	... Bombay, Punjab, Sind.
Wheat : Oct. to Dec. (sowing) —March to May (harvesting).	Lahore, Punjab, Bombay, Sind, U. P., Bihar, N. W. F. P., C.P., Ajmer-Merwara, Delhi.

Barley : Oct.—Nov. (sowing) Allahabad.
      March-April (harvest-
      ing).

Tin	...	Tavoy, Burma.
Myrobalam	...	Bimlipatam, Madras.
Wool	...	Hissar, Beawar, Fazilka.
Manganese	...	Vizagapatam, Madras.
Oats	...	Hissar, Punjab.
Lentils	...	C.P., Bihar.
Gram, Maize, Poppy Seed	...	U.P.

Groundnut : May to July ··· Madras, Bombay, C.P.,
     (sowing)—Sept. to   Orissa.
     Jan. (harvesting).

Rape & Mustard Seed : Aug. ...Cawnpore, Bihar, Bom-
     to Nov. (sowing)—Jan. bay, Punjab, U. P., &c.
     to April (harvesting).

Linseed : Aug. to Nov.   ... Bengal, Madras, Bom-
     (sowing)—Jan. to   bay, U.P., &c.
     April (harvesting).

Castor Seed : May to July or··· Bombay, Madras, C.P.,
     Sept. to Nov. (sowing) Sind, U.P.
     —Jan. to Feb. or
     March to April (har-
     vesting).

Copra   ...   Madras.

Tea : Seeds sown between West Duars, Sibsagar,
     Nov. and March and Bengal, Assam, Madras.
     seedlings transplanted
     when at least 6
     months old (sowing)

9

—May to Dec. (har-
vesting) in Northern
India and Jan. to Dec.
in Southern India.

Coffee : Rainy season (sowing) Madras, Orissa, Coorg.
—Oct. to April
(harvesting).

Sugarcane : Feb. to May ⋯   Bengal, Madras, Bombay,
(sowing)—Nov. to   Sind, U.P., Bihar, Orissa,
April (harvesting).   Punjab, C. P., Assam,
                N.W. F. P., Delhi.

CHAPTER XVI

General Considerations

Before making an attempt to forecast any market for any particular commodity, you should be very familiar with the nature of each sign of the zodiac, the influence of each planet in each sign, whether it is strong, weak or neutral in that sign and also the nature of the aspect it receives from other planets or it casts to other signs. All these you can easily ascertain from a study of any good book on Astrology.

Each commodity has its individual ruling sign and planet, as for example, Wheat is ruled by Taurus and Mercury, but as the sign and the planet also rule other commodities, the prices of all these commodities move in a similar curve. Also it is to be noted that some industries and commodities are so closely allied in the nature of their work that a rise of value in one necessarily involves a corresponding advance in the other ; thus, if the Iron Industry be stimulated by demands for construction works the Coal Trade will benefit from the employment of coal in Iron manufacture. These trades are united by the bond of co-operation to a common end, so that the influences which affect the one will include the other within their scope. It consists supply of effects produced in two industries by a common cause. Similarly, if the price of wheat rises, potatoes rise and other substitutive foods concurrently and gradually rise in sympathy.

This is simply due to the fact that people would not continue buying wheat, flour or rice at a higher price, when they can obtain a good alternative food in the form of potatoes or other articles at a cheaper price.

The commodities ruled by the Signs and Planets have already been given in a previous chapter.

The transits of the planets in the signs of the zodiac and the aspects they form with or receive from other planets while passing through the sign or the good or evil aspect they form with other signs of the zodiac will indicate the price fluctuations according to the nature of the aspects.

Planets are always strongest in their own signs, some better when exalted, and are weak in the signs of their detriment and fall. Planets are very often weak when retrograde.

If a planet is retrograde and receives a good aspect from another planet, it has very little effect, but if the latter planet receives also a good aspect from another planet, the aspect may have a very strong effect, generally for an advance. Thus, Jupiter or Uranus either retrograde or in evil aspect to one another and another planet, say Mars or Sun, is in good aspect to one of them makes a very strong grain market and gives some strength to the particular commodity or stock groups ruled by Jupiter or Uranus, which is called the Indicator of the particular kind of commodity or stock.

An Indicator is strong in its own sign. Thus, Sun in Leo is strong for Gold and when afflicted by one of the major planets the price of Gold is affected ; and in good aspects, the price advances ; so also when a major planet is in Leo and in evil aspect with other planets the price of Gold is affected, whereas good aspects enhance the price.

The natural effect of each planet in each sign can be determined by noting the effects of the Moon's aspects to that planet as it enters the sign. Thus, for example, when Jupiter enters the sign Taurus, the good aspects including the conjunction of the Moon cause advances in wheat prices.

It is by judging the effects of combined aspects of the larger planets that show what the market will be. Note that even when the Sun may have no aspects whatever, the aspects of the two or three planets will be apparent most of the time, if more than three, in addition to the Moon, the influence will be very marked.

There are periods when there are no close aspects between the planets for several days. You will be in doubt and uncertain and at such times you will be wise to stay out of the markets, as there are plenty of periods when there are good aspects to buy and evil aspects to sell.

An alternation from a higher to a lower price level or *vice versa*, is generally observed when a new or full Moon happens near about the apogee or perigee. This will be found very useful in determining the highest or lowest points touched in a month in conformity with the principal planetary configurations.

CHAPTER XVII

Charting the Price Fluctuations

In every commodity there is a seasonal change in prices. If you take the price records of say, 10 or 12 years for a commodity and make an average of the prices month by month and week by week, you will obtain the *norm* of the price chart of the commodity week by week. Below this chart draw a straight line representing this norm and divide this line into as many equal sections as shall represent months and weeks over which your observations are required to extend, and against the sections put the dates of the month thus indicated.

As the fluctuations of price depend on the aspects of the planets, note from the Ephemeris all the aspects formed by the planets, their positions in the signs of the zodiac during the concerned period and place the good aspects above the line and the evil aspects underneath the line of norm, but always observing to place each aspect in the perpendicular of that date on which it is formed. You may now take a pencil and starting from your earliest date draw a

line upwards or downwards, as the case may be, to the
first of the aspect formed, proceeding to the next
aspect upwards, if the aspect is a good one, or downwards, when the aspect is an evil one, and so on. You
will then have a zigzag line crossing the norm at
irregular intervals.

This represents your curve and it will indicate with
great precision the rise or fall which takes place in
the price of the concerned commodity on the open
market. But it should be noted that all the aspects
are not of equal value and also the influence of all
the planets are not of equal potence. Consequently
some considerations are to be made in drawing the
curve. Each planet acts in its own way. In raising
the value of commodities Jupiter has the greatest
influence, next to it Venus, then Mars, Neptune,
Uranus and Saturn. In depressing the value, Saturn
has the greatest influence, then Uranus, Jupiter and
Neptune. It may therefore be found advisable to
place the aspects nearer or further from the Line of
Norm according as may be the influence of the planets
which form the aspect. Thus, a good aspect of Jupiter
would raise the market more than a good aspect of
Saturn, and similarly an evil aspect of Saturn would
depress the market more than an evil aspect of Mars.

A movement extends from the beginning to the
end of a rise or a fall. Hence, it is necessary, in order
to determine the duration of movements, to take the
middle date between any two aspects.

A boom on the market is caused by a succession of

good aspects to the concerned planet ruling the particular commodity or produce, without any intervening evil aspects to break the series. A slump is the result of a succession of evil aspects to the concerned planet without any intervening good aspects to break the series.

A change from up to down or the reverse is usually indicated by a change in the nature of the ephemeral aspects received by the concerned ruling planet or Indicator of the commodity or produce.

Thus, if you find a succession of good aspects to the Indicator and then a series of evil aspects or mixed ones, a change takes place when the planet moves from one to the other. This date is called the Transition Date. It is fixed by taking the date of the last good or bad aspect and the next bad or good aspect to the Indicator counting the number of days and dividing by two, which, being added to the first date, gives the *date of transition*. An interval of at least three or four days between two sorts of aspects should be allowed so that the Indicator may clear the last influence by its ephemeral motion before entering upon the next.

These are the general principles which will indicate accurately the fluctuations of prices when ordinary crop conditions prevail without any political strain. Abnormal movements are likely to occur when conditions are otherwise than normal as are produced in the market by abnormal factors generally called artificial factors, such as Wars, Plagues, Strikes, &c.

CHAPTER XVIII

Wheat Market

Mercury is said to be the Significator of cereals generally. The sign Virgo and the planet Mercury will affect the fluctuations of Wheat Market.

First of all calculate the Line of Norm or the normal price curve representing the average value for each month or week from the records of a number of past years, which will show the times at which the price of wheat is higher than at others, owing to crop seasons. All the fluctuations of prices will be in reference to this Norm line.

The fluctuation of price depends on the good and bad aspects of Mercury and other modifying conditions are denoted by the transits of the planets in several signs of the zodiac.

The signs are grouped into elements, Fire, Earth, Air and Water. The earthy signs are most favourable for wheat, next the watery signs, then the airy and lastly the fiery signs. The passage of Mercury through these signs and the aspects it receives from other planets generally show the tone of the market. The passage of the other planets through the signs Virgo and Taurus will modify the tone of the market from the nature of the planet and the aspects it receives during its passage through these signs. Also the good or evil aspects a planet casts from other signs to these signs will have modifying effects on the produce and price of the article to some extent. When Mercury passes through the earthy signs and also receives good aspects from other planets the price of wheat rises, and proportionately less so when it passes through the signs of other elements. When it receives evil aspects the price falls.

The trine and sextile aspects of all planets and the conjunction of Venus and Jupiter are good, and the opposition, square, semisquare and sesquiquadrate (135 deg.) aspects of all planets and the conjunctions of Saturn, Uranus and Neptune are bad. The conjunction of Mars generally brings a sharp rise but often not a lasting one, and sometimes it indicates a fall according to the position and strength of the planet. The effects of the aspects of Pluto have not yet been fully determined but generally its nature is judged similar to Mars and Uranus.

A good aspect indicates a rise and an evil aspect, a fall. But the aspects of all planets are not of equal value. In raising the price of wheat Venus has the greatest influence and next to it is Jupiter, then Mars, Neptune, Uranus and Saturn. In depressing the price, consequently Saturn has the greatest influence, next to it comes Uranus, then Neptune, Mars and Jupiter. Thus a good aspect of Venus would raise the market more than a good aspect of Saturn, and similarly a bad aspect of Saturn would depress the market more than a bad aspect of Mars.

The parallel of declination between the planets is only to be considered when it is of the same denomination, that is, both are North or both South. It will then act like a conjunction and the influence will act for several days.

The conjunction of Sun and Mercury generally brings a change in the trend of the market. The aspects of the Moon are ephemeral and last only for a few hours, and are therefore generally not considered.

Ascertain from an Ephemeris the month in which Mercury receives the greater number of consecutive good aspects. This will give the month in which the price will be higher in relation to the Norm. Similarly ascertain the month in which the planet has the greatest number of evil aspects, which will show the month of the lowest price than the Norm. Mixed aspects will bring ups and downs according to the nearest dates of their formation. All these, of course, are modified by the transits of the other planets in several signs of the zodiac and their aspects to the signs Virgo and Taurus.

The daily fluctuations of the market are therefore to be ascertained from the aspects of Mercury and other planets as explained above.

The period of a boom or a slump will depend on the succession of consecutive good or evil aspects of the planet, and when there is a gap between the aspects of the intermediate dates, the middle date between the last good or bad aspect and the next bad or good aspect is to be taken for the date of actual change in the price as has already been explained in the previous chapter.

CHAPTER XIX

Sugar Market

The sign Aries and its ruler Mars indicate the produce and supply of Sugar. Consequently the second sign Taurus and its ruler control the price.

Plentitude or scarcity of supply is therefore indicated by the position of Mars in the particular zodiacal sign and also from the aspects it receives from other planets.

Mars is strong in the signs Aries, Scorpio and Capricorn and when in these signs, there will be plenty of supply, if through its passage in these signs it receives good aspects ; but if the aspects are bad the supply is restricted.

Mars is weak in the signs, Taurus, Cancer and Libra and when it passes through these signs and is badly aspected it will show a corresponding scarcity of sugar.

In other signs proportionate increase of supply is denoted by good aspects and corresponding want of supply is indicated by evil aspects.

The cause of dearth of supply may be ascertained from the nature of the aspecting planet. Uranus in evil aspects shows restrictions of supply through Government interferences or some other action of the authorities at the ports or factories. Neptune in evil aspects shows cliques or some action of speculators making a "corner" in the article. The evil aspects of Saturn generally indicate bad crop reports, and the evil aspects of Jupiter indicate troubles from speculators. On the other hand, good aspects of the major planets show easy supplies.

Also the position of Mars in its aphelion in the early degrees of Virgo shows an easy supply and correspondingly its position in its perihelion in the early degrees of Pisces shows scarcity in supply. The position of Venus in its aphelion in Libra 10° brings an easy market and its position in its perihelion in Aries 10°, brings a rise in price. Abnormal conditions indicated by the aspects of the other planets, of course, modify these indications.

The price fluctuations are indicated by the position of Venus in signs and its aspects to other planets.

Venus is strong in Taurus, Cancer, Libra and Pisces. When Venus is in any of these signs and is in good aspects with the major planets the price will rise. Venus is weak in Aries, Virgo, Scorpio and Capricorn and consequently when it is in any of these signs and in good aspects to other planets the price will not rise to the same extent as when it is in a congenial sign ; and a proportionate rise in price will be shown when it is in any of the other signs and in good aspects to the major planets. Similarly evil aspects, when the planet is in its weak signs, will bring a marked fall in price than when it is in any of its strong signs or proportionately so when in any of the other signs.

An average norm line of price values should be prepared from past records of several years and the the fluctuations of price should be referred to this chart according to the positions and aspects of both Mars and Venus.

First, the aspects of Mars should be noted and set against the day of the month from the Ephemeris. This will give the indication of the condition of supply.

Next, note similarly the aspects of Venus as they occur from day to day and also note the change of signs of both the planets that may occur in the course of the period for which the chart is made.

From these two sets of aspects a common curve can be drawn which will indicate the rise and fall of prices.

A boom is caused when good aspects of the two planets, particularly that of Venus, are continuous without any intervening bad aspects to break the series. Similarly a slump is the result of a succession of bad aspects, particularly to Venus, without any intervening good aspects. When Venus comes in conjunction with the Sun generally a change from up to down or the reverse is shown, but more reliable results are shown by the change from a good to a bad aspect of the planet.

Transition dates will fall as usual, midway between the last good or bad aspects and the next bad or good ones, and the interval between these dates to be allowed has already been explained in Chapter XVII.

CHAPTER XX

Rice Market

In considering the Rice Market we must note that the market generally depends on the produce of the crops in India, Burma and China, but India and Burma rule the market chiefly. Capricorn rules India and the fourth sign from this is Aries, which would naturally indicate the produce of this country.

Aries is ruled by Mars and therefore this planet is the indicator of this market. Therefore the position and aspects of Mars will show the fluctuations in the market.

Mars is strong in Aries, Scorpio and Capricorn, hence when Mars is in one of these signs and receives good aspects of the major planets, the market will show a rise, but evil aspects will show the contrary though not in a very marked way. When Mars is in Taurus, Cancer or Libra, the signs of its detriment, and receives evil aspects, the market will show a marked downward tendency, but contrary aspects will produce a moderate rise ; and when Mars is in any other signs, the fluctuations will be accordingly to the general nature of the aspects it receives. The modifying factors are the planets which transit the signs Capricorn and Aries or which aspects these signs, a good aspect indicating a rise, and a bad, a fall.

In considering the rice market, the seasonal rise and fall should be considered by the Norm curve calculated from the average of the price fluctuations for several past years. Every year there is at one time a low price period and at other, a higher price period according to the time of new crops, but whether this rise or fall will be marked or not, should be judged by the harvest indications and the position of Mars and its aspects for the concerned period. The condition of harvest is judged from the Sun's entry into the cardinal signs for India, Burma and China according to the rules of Mundane Astrology explained in a previous chapter of this book.

For the fluctuations of price take the position of Mars and its aspects and consider whether its position is strong or weak ; note the dates on which it forms the several aspects in their order during a month and draw your conclusions exacly as if you are dealing with the planet for Wheat or Sugar.

CHAPTER XXI

Cotton Market

The Cotton Market depends on more than one factor. Besides the position and aspects of the planets ruling this commodity, the horoscopes of the chief centres of Cotton Industry are also to be considered.

The chief cotton sphere lies across the Southern States of America with its centre at New Orleans. The horoscope of this place has Gemini 27° on the Ascendant and Pisces 3° on the Mid-heaven. Therefore Virgo 3° is on the lower meridian and Sagittarious 27° is on the Descendant. Also the other principal centres are New York, Liverpool and Bombay, etc., and the horoscope cast for each day at noon for any of these places with which you are dealing, will be necessary for noting on what days during a month any planets transit the Significators of the horoscope and their opposition points. Also similar considerations are to be made in respect of the horoscopes of the Stock Exchange for these places, which have been already given in a previous chapter of this book.

The chief Significators are the Mid-heaven, Ascendant, the Sun and the Moon. The transits over these four Significators are to be considered. Oppositions to these Significators are always depressing.

The planets in transits are considered according to their nature and the aspects received by them at the

10

time of transits. The transits of the benefic planets or the good aspects of the planets to the Significators tend to raise the price, while transits of the evil planets or the evil aspects of the planets tend to bring a fall.

A planet in transit must be free from aspects of other planets to be judged by itself alone according to its nature. But if it receives good aspects it produces a rise and if it is badly aspected, it produces a fall when in transit over the daily horoscope.

The effects of all the planets, however, are not same. Jupiter, Venus, Mercury or Moon (well aspected) produces a rise. Mars well aspected brings a sudden rise. Uranus and Saturn generally bring falls ; so also any planet afflicted at transit.

As the Sun always transits the Mid-heaven every day at noon, his aspects on the day are, of course, the determining factor. Also when a New Moon or a Full Moon happens when the Moon comes to its apogee or perigee a change in the price often occurs, either the highest or the lowest price for the month is touched about these dates.

The crops are to be judged from Virgo and the planets that pass through it or aspect it, and also from the aspects they receive during their transits in this sign.

When either the sign Virgo or the planet transiting or aspecting the sign receives good aspects from other planets, particularly benefics, good crops are assured, but when the aspects are bad, particularly from evil planets, crops will fail and generally there will be a rise in price.

Fluctuations in price are to be judged similarly from the sign Libra, and the planets passing through that sign or aspecting it, according to the nature of the aspects they receive.

In determining the rise and fall in prices, first see if the Mid-heaven, Ascendant and their opposite points in the Cotton horoscope are in any way affected by the transits or aspects of any planets.

Next see on what days during the concerned period any planets transit or aspect the Significators of the daily horoscopes cast for noon for the place of the particular Cotton Industry centre, such as, New York, Liverpool, Bombay, etc., with which you are dealing and also see if any planets transit or aspect the Significators of the Stock Exchange Horoscope of that place.

Now see whether there are any planets in Virgo or Libra and also the aspects they receive during their stay therein. Also see if any planets aspect any of these signs.

These indications control the major factors of price fluctuations and are the primary features of the tone of the market.

Finally take out from the Ephemeris the aspects to Mercury for crop condition and those to Venus for price variations from day to day.

A combined consideration of all these factors will determine the rise and fall in price.

Mercury and Venus are the chief aspect making planets and their aspects should be carefully noted for daily fluctuations. Venus in Virgo and Mercury in Libra steady the cotton market. But when Mercury or Venus is retrograde or any retrograde planet is posited in Libra the price falls.

It would be better to prepare a chart for the average price fluctuations for every week or so from past price records for several years, say five, and consider this as the Norm line of seasonal variations in price, and the fluctuations indicated from the consideration of all the above planetary influences should be taken in relation to this norm, as are done in the case of other commodities.

Good aspects mean a rise in price and bad aspects, a fall. Conjunctions act differently according to the nature of the planet involved. Jupiter, Venus and Mercury, when their last aspects are benefic, produce a rise. Saturn and Uranus, particularly when connected with Venus or Libra, bring a fall, the one steadily, the other sporadically. Mars, especially in connection with Venus or Libra, is capable of stimulating the market so as to produce a sharp rise or a fall according to its position in the particular sign of the zodiac, and to the aspects it receives from other planets.

When there are no planets found in Virgo or Libra, consider the transits and aspects to the significators of the above horoscopes ; but when all these are absent, judge the fluctuations of the market from the joint ephemeral aspects of Venus and Mercury. The general rule is to consider all the factors before a rise or a fall is estimated.

As in other commodities a succession of good aspects gives a "boom" and a succession of bad aspects, a "slump". But they must be consecutive and not interrupted by cross aspects to produce these results. The midway point between good and bad aspects indicates a "turn" in the market price.

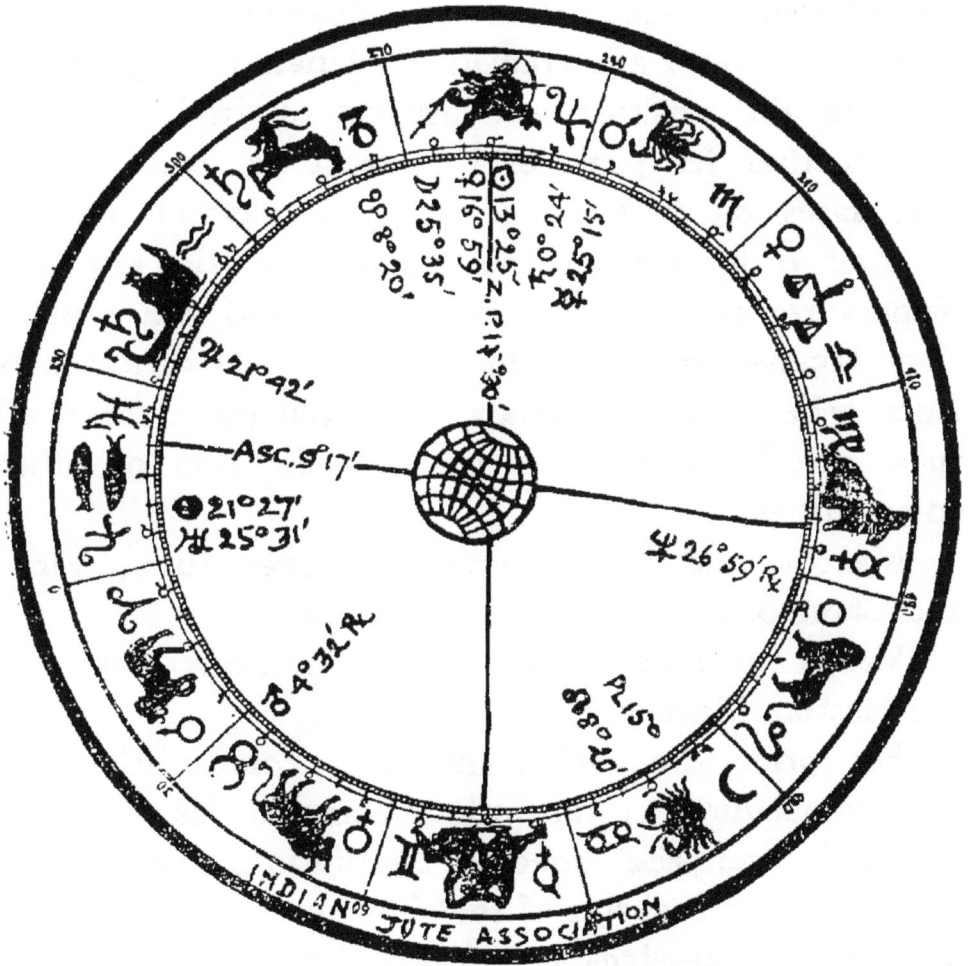

CHAPTER XXII

Rubber, Jute and Hessian Market

Like all other commodities a Chart of Norm is to be prepared and fluctuations in price are to be considered in relation to this.

For the Rubber Market the general principles are the same as governing the wheat or sugar market, but the specific fluctuations are judged from ephemeral aspects of Jupiter and transits of planets in Sagittarius.

Take the position and aspects of Jupiter. Conder whether its position is strong or weak, note the dates on which it forms the several aspects in their order during the month, and also see what planets transit the sign Sagittarius and the aspects they receive, or the sign itself receives the aspects from other planets. Draw your conclusions from all these exactly as you do in the consideration of other commodities.

Mercury and Saturn have rule over Jute; Virgo and Capricorn have also connection with it.

Venus and Libra, Uranus and Aquarius stand for the Hessian Market.

For price fluctuations in these commodities, the same procedure as for other commodities is to be followed and the specific fluctuations are judged from ephemeral aspects of the above planets and transits of planets in the signs mentioned above.

The fluctuations of prices in Jute (raw) and also the condition of the Jute Market can be also determined from the aspects and transits of the planets in the horoscope of the Indian Jute Association, registered on the 6th Dec. 1926 at Calcutta (Page 149), or of Calcutta Jute Exchange, registered on the 11-9-1936, or the East Indian Jute Association, registered on the 2-6-1927, Calcutta ; or better a consideration of all the three horoscopes should be made.

Similarly for the Hessian Market the transits of the planets in the horoscope of Calcutta Hessian Exchange, registered on the 3-4-1929, Calcutta, will show the trend of the market.

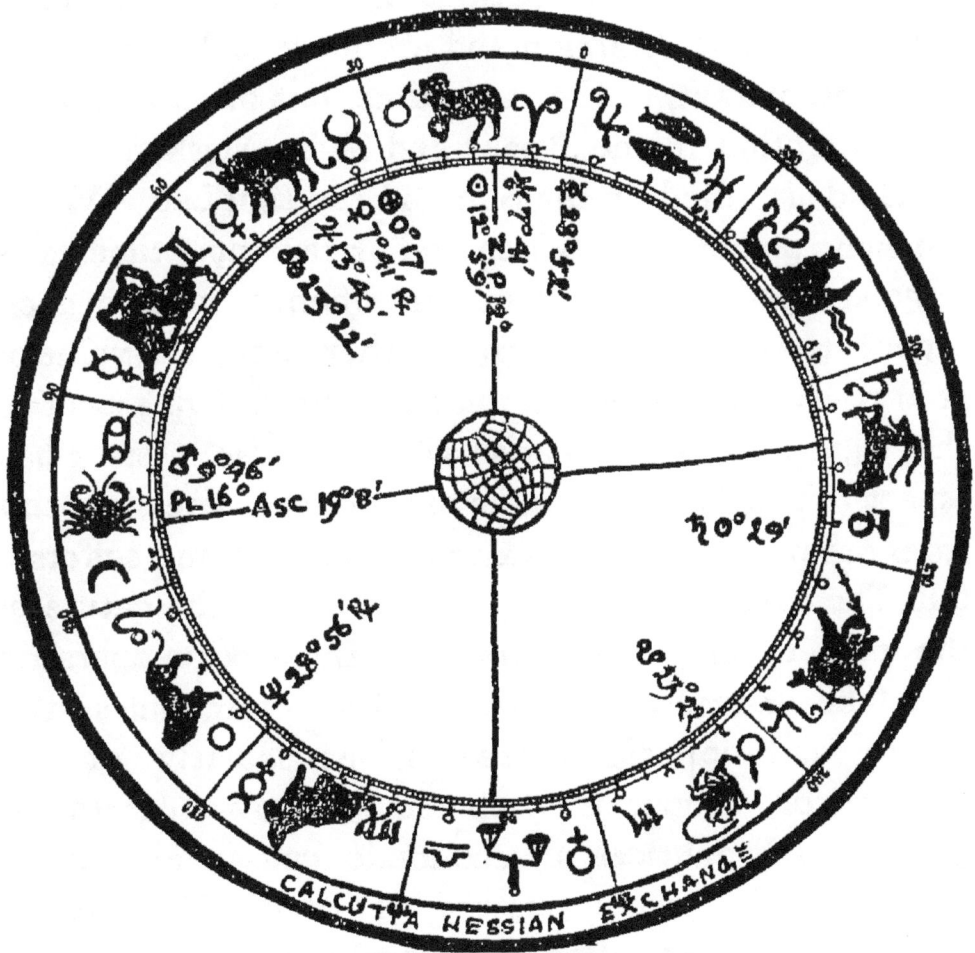

CALCUTTA HESSIAN EXCHANGE

CHAPTER XXIII

The Bullion Market

The movements of the Bullion Market are indicated mostly by the general aspects between the four larger planets of the Solar System. They show or indicate the tendency for long periods.

Gold and Silver have their individual ruling signs and planets, but as a rule their value fluctuations move in sympathy with the fluctuations of other vital commodities in the same direction and are more or less active in an active market, at the same time, but often in a contrary direction 'to the Stocks and Share Market.

Gold is ruled by the Sun and the sign Leo. When a benefic planet transits Leo and at the same time casts a good aspect to the Sun, or when it casts a good aspect to the sign Leo from other signs, the value of gold rises. But when a planet casts an evil aspect to the sign Leo, particularly when it also casts a bad aspect to the Sun at the same time or receives evil aspects from other planets, the value depreciates and suffers a fall. The extent of rise or fall depends on the nature of the planets and the nature of the aspects operating with the concerned planet. But sometimes the square and opposition aspects, particularly of evil planets or superior planets, show dearth of gold through political or economic causes and bring a rise in the value instead of a fall. The transit of Mars in Leo often produces a temporary rise or fall according to the nature of aspects it receives and also to the nature of the aspecting planet. The transits of Saturn in Leo and the Sun in the ruling signs of Saturn or in good aspect with Saturn, bring a rise, particularly when Saturn is retrograde. The effects of Saturn is of a lasting nature. From the above it is therefore clear that planets, especially the evil planets, transiting Leo, Taurus, Scorpio or Aquarius, show rise in gold-value according to the nature of the aspects received from other planets during their transits, particularly when they are retrograde. An evil aspect generally hampers the rise. Sometimes the transits of benefic planets show easy market, while those of evil planets bring political and economic troubles and create demand for gold, consequently bringing a rise in value. All these are more clearly ascertained from the Ingress maps of a country.

The transits of the Sun in its congenial signs, such as Aries and Leo, bring a rise, particularly when it receives good aspects from other planets, but the evil aspects will cause a temporary depression. But when the Sun passes through the signs of its detriment, such as Libra and Aquarius, the value is depressed according to the evil aspects it receives from other planets, while the good aspects will bring a somewhat steady value but not a very marked rise. Much will also depend on the nature and strength of the aspecting planet.

For the daily fluctuations of gold value, ephemeral aspects of all planets. to the Sun and to the sign Leo should be considered according to the nature of the aspects and to the strength or weakness of the aspecting planet. The fluctuations are to be judged from the combined influences of these indications and those of the general aspects between the major planets.

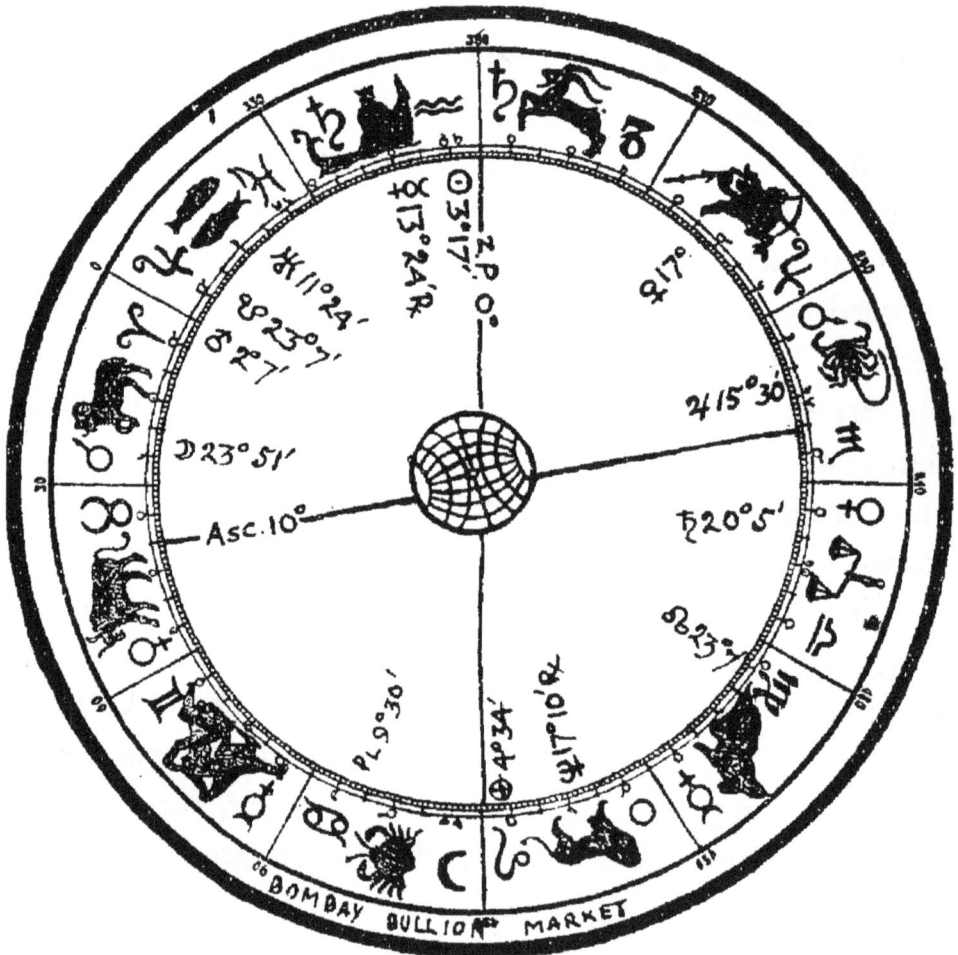

BOMBAY BULLION MARKET

In India the fluctuations in the Bullion Market are also indicated by the transits and aspects of the major planets in the cardinal houses of the horoscope of the Bombay Bullion Market. This market was established at Bombay on the 24th January,

1923. The horoscope for noon at Bombay on this date shows 0° Aquarius was culminating (Zenith Point) and the 10th degree of Taurus was rising. The map is given above.

For example, on the 26th January, 1947, Mars transited the Zenith Point of this horoscope and the price of gold began to rise steadily, and on the 7th February, Mars came to the square of the Ascendant, and the price began to fall. On the 4th June, Mars transited the Ascendant, and the price of gold began to rise steadily. During 1948 both Saturn and Mars transited the sign Leo and in March both these planets transited the 4th cardinal house of this horoscope and in square aspect to Jupiter and in trine to the Moon of this horoscope, there was a steady rise in the price of gold. During 1946—48 Saturn passed through Leo and received in 1948 the trine aspects of Jupiter and the price rose considerably and was the highest ever recorded in the past. The price of silver, however, did not rise to the same extent, though there was a rise and the market was steady in sympathy. It is therefore advisable to consider the transits in this map when considering the price fluctuations of gold and silver.

The chief centre of Silver Market is Mexico. Its ruling sign is Capricorn and its ruler, Saturn. The fluctuations of price depend much on these. Also Mercury, and to some extent Moon and Venus, cause minor fluctuations from day to day.

Cancer, however, is the chief ruling sign of silver

and Mercury is the chief ruling planet. Saturn and Capricorn act only in a secondary way. As the ruler of Cancer the Moon has some effect on it, but she is not a particular significator of anything. Her passage through Cancer or Capricorn may stimulate the price, but not always in accordance with the nature of the aspects received during her passages through these signs. The position of the Moon in its orbit, however, has a general influence on fluctuations, especially in regard to changes from an upward to a downward movement, and *vice versa*. This is very marked in the case of the Moon's passage over its apogee and perigee, particularly if a new or a full moon happens at that time.

Mercury and Saturn generally denote a rise or a fall in value according to their aspects with other planets and to the signs congenial or uncongenial to their nature, through which they pass at the time. The Moon's passage through its favourable or unfavorable signs confirms or retards these influences, but the ephemeral aspects of the Moon have very little control over the price fluctuations.

When a planet passes through Cancer or Capricorn the price of silver fluctuates according to the nature of the aspects it receives. Similar effects also happen when a planet aspects these signs favourably or unfavourably, but in a general way according to the nature of the planet and also to the nature of the aspects it receives from other planets at the same time.

For examples, when a planet is in Aries, it will be in evil aspect to both Cancer and Capricorn and will generally depress the price of silver, particularly if it receives an evil aspect from an evil planet ; but when it receives a good aspect, particularly from a benefic planet, it will prevent a considerable fall. The transit of a benefic planet brings a rise, while that of a malefic planet. a fall, depending much on the nature of the aspects received by it.

During 1915-17 Saturn passed through Cancer and obtained benefic aspects of Jupiter and the price of silver rose considerably. In 1921—23 Saturn in Libra in square aspect with the ruling sign of Mexico and also Jupiter in 1922 badly aspecting Capricorn, brought a slump in the silver market. Again in 1944 to 1946 Saturn passed through Cancer and Leo, and was well aspected by Jupiter, the price of silver rose to famine figure.

For the general fluctuations in silver values, we should look to Mercury and its ephemeral aspects. When Mercury enters Cancer or Capricorn and is favourably aspected by the planets, particularly by benefic ones, the price will rise, but if in evil aspects, particularly with malefic planets, or Mercury is retrograde, the price will fall. Generally the aspects of Jupiter, Uranus, Mars, Venus and Neptune bring a rise and of Saturn bring a fall. When Mercury is in good aspects, conjunction or in a parallel declination. of the same denomination with benefic planets, the price rises and evil aspects and conjunction with an evil planet will bring a fall.

When in other signs which are in sextile or trine to Cancer or Capricorn, Mercury will bring a rise according to the benefic aspects from other planets. But when in square or other evil aspects to these signs the fall will be more prominent from the evil aspects of other planets and the rise will be less marked even when it receives good aspects. For example, when Mercury is in Aries or Libra, an evil aspect will bring more marked fall than when it receives a good aspect.

When a benefic planet transits these signs or throws a good aspect to them as well as to the Moon, when the latter passes through these signs, the price rises. Similarly, evil aspects will bring a fall. When an evil planet passes through these signs or throws evil aspects to them as well as to the Moon, when the latter passes through these signs, the price falls.

According to Varaha Mihira Mars rules gold and Jupiter rules silver. It will therefore be interesting to note how the transits and aspects of these two planets affect the Bullion Market. On the 16th June, 1947, Mars was in opposition to Jupiter and the price of silver fell gradually up to the middle of July and from the 21st July there were successions of good aspects to Jupiter and the price began to rise again. On the 20th August, Mars was in sesquiquadrate aspect to Jupiter and the price began to fall steadily up to the third week of October in spite of the trine aspect of

Mars on the 20th September, for, in the Ingress map of the autumnal equinox, Jupiter was in the 4th house heavily afflicted by Saturn rising, and was in conjunction with the South Node !

For both gold and silver values, the conjunctions of the Sun, Venus and Jupiter are good. The sextile and trine are good of all planets. The square and opposition are bad aspects and also semi-square and sesquiquadrate (135°) are bad. Conjunctions with Jupiter, Mars and Uranus often give a rise due to some abnormal conditions, but the conjunction of Saturn always depresses the market. Neptune and Venus bring moderate results. The aspects of Pluto have effects on the value according to the nature of the aspects but in a moderate degree. A good aspect will bring a rise, and an evil aspect, a fall. The Sun and the Moon do not bring marked results by themselves except under particular conditions stated above.

CHAPTER XXIV

Ephemeral Price Fluctuation

Besides the considerations of the Ingress and Lunation figures and other principal factors for the price fluctuations of commodities, ephemeral planetary aspects among themselves will show in a general way the daily trend of rise and fall in the market of any particular commodity according to the aspects or configurations of the planet or planets ruling the commodity.

In the following examples the trend of prices of a few principal commodities is shown for the period April to June, 1925. It will be easily evident from the charts and the planetary configurations that the planets do not affect the market in a sporadic manner but in a definite and consistent way and the inhibition of their effects occurs only when contradictory configurations or strong influence of other factors opposing their action are present at the same time or period.

The Important daily planetary aspects for the above period were :

April, 1925.

1. Venus 135° Neptune and sextile Mars ; Mars 135° Jupiter. 5. Mercury parallel Neptune. 6. Venus parallel Uranus. 10. Sun trine Neptune ; Mercury

parallel Neptune. 11. Sun square Jupiter. 13. Venus trine Neptune. 14. Venus square Jupiter. 16. Mercury semi-square Mars. 17. Mercury parallel Saturn. 18. Sun conjunction Mercury. 19. Mercury conjunction Venus. 20. Sun parallel Mercury. 21. Mercury parallel Venus, 23. Mars sextile Neptune. 24. Sun conjunction Venus, parallel Saturn. 26. Venus semi-square Mars, parallel Saturn. 28. Sun semi-square Mars ; Venus semi-square Uranus ; Mercury sextile Mars. 29. Sun semi-square Uranus ; Mercury square Jupiter. 30. Venus opposition Saturn ; Mars square Uranus.

May, 1925.

1. Sun opposition Saturn. 2. Sun parallel Neptune and Venus ; Venus parallel Neptune. 3. Mars 135° Saturn. 5. Mercury square Jupiter. 7. Venus square Neptune. 9. Venus trine Jupiter. 11. Sun square Neptune ; Venus sextile Uranus. 13. Sun trine Jupiter. 16. Sun sextile Uranus. 17. Mars semi-square Neptune. 18. Saturn 135° Uranus. 21. Venus 135° Jupiter. 22. Venus parallel Jupiter. 24. Mercury opposition Saturn ; Mars trine Saturn. 25. Mercury semi-square Uranus, parallel Saturn, sextile Mars. 28. Sun 135° Jupiter. 30. Sun parallel Jupiter. 31. Mercury parallel Neptune ; Venus sextile Neptune.

June, 1925.

1. Mercury square Neptune. 2. Mercury trine Jupiter. 3. Venus 135° Saturn, parallel Mars. 4. Mercury sextile Uranus. 5. Venus square Uranus. 8. Mercury semi-square Mars. 9. Mercury 135° Jupiter. 10. Sun sextile Neptune, parallel Mars ; Mars opposition Jupiter.

11

12. Mercury parallel Jupiter. 13. Venus semi-square Neptune. 14. Sun 135° Saturn ; Mercury parallel Mars. 15. Sun parallel Mercury ; Venus trine Saturn. 16. Mercury sextile Neptune. 17. Sun square Uranus ; Mercury 135° Saturn. 18. Mercury square Uranus, parallel Venus. 19. Mars trine Uranus. 20. Sun conjunction Mercury ; Mars parallel Jupiter. 23. Sun parallel Venus ; Mercury semi-square Neptune. 24. Mercury trine Saturn. 25. Venus opposition Jupiter. 27. Sun semi-square Neptune. 29. Mercury opposition Jupiter ; Venus trine Uranus. 30. Sun trine Saturn ; Venus parallel Jupiter.

Chart I. Wheat Market

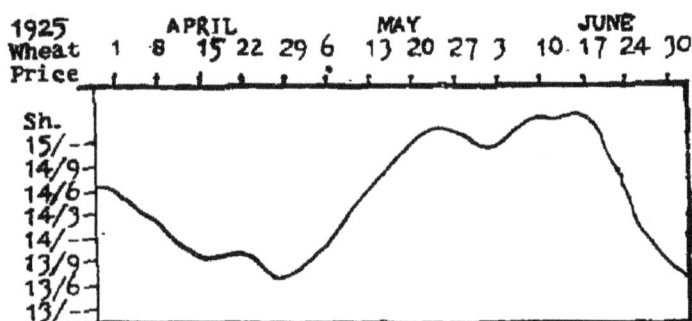

Venus rules this market. Throughout the month of April Venus had evil aspects and up to the 15th a steady fall was found. From the 15th to 22nd the market remained steady due to Mercury conjunction Venus, but after that the evil aspects of Venus indicated a further fall and reached the lowest level for the month on the 29th due to Venus opposition Saturn.

The month of May shows considerable good

aspects of Venus and in spite of the square of Neptune on the 7th and a minor 135° to Jupiter on the 21st the market rose steadily up to about the 27th. During June there were preponderance of evil aspects to Venus, except a trine aspect to Saturn on the 15th and the market fell in the first week but rose a little in the second week, remaining steady between 10th and 17th, then again fell due to opposition of Jupiter on the 25th. The trine of Uranus on the 29th had no practical effect for this month.

Chart II. Steel Market

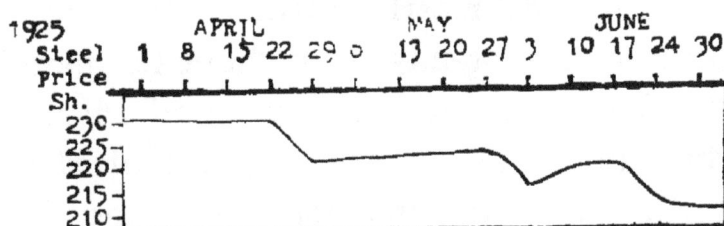

This market is chiefly ruled by Mars. The configurations of this planet during April were generally evil and weak, but the good aspects on the 1st by sextile Venus and on the 23rd by sextile Neptune kept the market steady without practically no fluctuations in price. The major evil aspect Mars square Uranus on the 30th brought a fall from 22nd to 29th.

The configurations of May were of minor importance and the good aspects Mars trine Saturn and sextile Mercury of the 24th and 25th kept the market steady without any noticeable fluctuations, but the evil aspects in the month of June, particularly the major

aspect opposition of Jupiter on the 11th brought a fall
about this period and kept the market low for the
period.

Chart III. Sugar Market

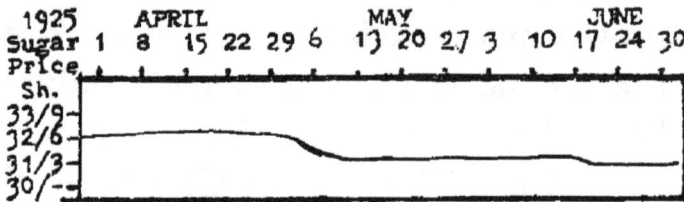

This market is chiefly ruled by the combined influence of Mars and Venus. The configurations of these
planets are minor and mostly mixed during April and
the market remained steady throughout the month, but
on the 30th Venus opposition Saturn and Mars square
Uranus brought a fall. The aspects of the these
planets during May and June were mixed and the major
good aspects kept the market steady without much
fluctuations.

Chart IV. Rubber Market

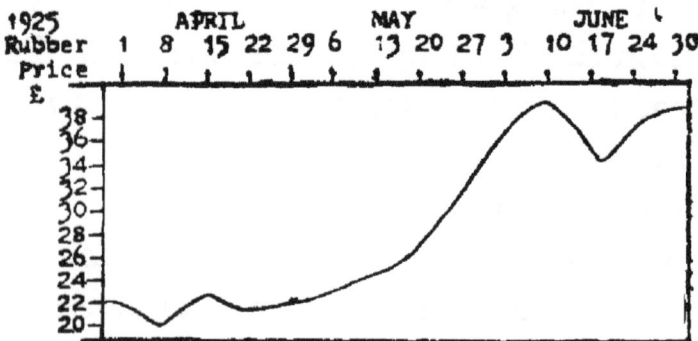

This market is ruled by Jupiter with sometimes a
sub-influence of Mars, which is generally ignored. The

aspects of Jupiter throughout the month of April were bad, and the price fell during this month. In May the majority of the aspects were strong and good except a few insignificant minor aspects towards the end, but in the first week of June there was the strong good aspect of Mercury trine Jupiter. The market rose steadily in May and up to the 10th June and fell in the middle of the month due to the evil aspect of Mars opposition Jupiter on the 11th and again rose from about the 17th due to the strong good aspect of Mars trine Uranus on the 19th.

Chart V.   Tea Market

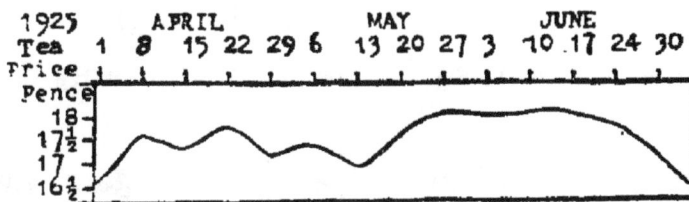

This market is ruled by Neptune and Mars. The beginning of April shows a few good aspects of Neptune and a few evil aspects of Mars up to the middle of this month. There were ups and downs in the market up to the 22nd and the evil major aspect Mars square Uranus brought a steady fall, which continued up to the middle of May, during which both Mars and Neptune had evil aspects only. During the latter part of May there were good aspects of both Neptune and Mars and the market rose and remained steady up to the first week of June and then there was a fall, as both these planets had evil aspects in June.

Chart VI.   Rice Market

In this example we consider the market condition for the period January to April, 1926.   This market is ruled by Mars.

1926 January 2nd Mars par. Jupiter
25th Mars semi-sq. Jupiter
30th Mars sq. Uranus
31st Mars trine Neptune

The market rose steadily from the first week and became dull towards the last week but recovered soon.

February 20th Mars 135° Neptune
24th Mars semi-sq. Saturn

After 17th the market fell steadily and at the end was considerably down.

1926 March, 16th Mars sextile Uranus
17th Mars sextile Saturn

The market again began to rise from the 17th and during the rest of the month the price was on the rise.

April, 8th Mars semi-sq. Uranus
17th Mars par. Saturn
22nd Mars opposition Neptune
23rd Mars conj. Jupiter
25th Mars square Saturn
28th Mars par. Jupiter

For the first half of the month the market was very bad, the price was falling and from the 21st the price fell considerably.   But from the 23rd the market took a decided turn towards good and it rose rapidly, though a slight depression was shown about the 25th.   Immediately after this date the market rose rapidly due to the parallel aspect of Jupiter.

Chart VII   Cotton Market

In this example we consider the market for the period of December, 1922 and January, 1923. The market is ruled by Venus and Mercury. During this period Saturn was in Libra, and was par. to Mars.

Date	Aspect in December, 1922.	N. Y. Quotations
4		24.35
6	Venus square Mars	24.26
9	Saturn sextile Mars	24.92
10	Saturn sextile Sun	
11	Saturn sextile Neptune	24.89
13		25.36
15	Mars transits opp. Asc. of Cotton Horoscope	25.23
	Mars transits Z. P. of Cotton Horoscope	25.44
18		25.80
20		25.75
22	Merc. semi-square Venus	
26		25.54
29	Merc. square Saturn	25.42
Date	Aspect in January, 1923.	N. Y. Quotation
3		25.58
	Merc. sextile Venus	26.42
		26.35

10		26.50
11	Sun square Saturn	
13	Venus par. Mars	27.53
15	Sun semi-square Venus	27.45
16		27.13
17	Venus square Uranus	
20	Venus sextile Merc.	28.15
24	Venus trine Neptune	28.35
27	Venus sextile Saturn	
29	Venus semi-square Mars	
30		27.95

In December, 1922 we find in the first week Venus square Mars, the price declined a little, but following it Saturn had many good aspects in succession from the 9th to the 11th and on the 16th Mars transited the Z. P. of the American Cotton Horoscope and the price rose 166 points, a boom so to speak, though Mercury's transit on the opposition of the ascendant of the Cotton horoscope on the 15th brought a slight temporary fall on that date. On the 23rd and 29th we have only bad aspects and accordingly from the middle point of these dates, that is, from the 26th we see a fall.

In January, 1923 Saturn par. Mars followed by Mercury sextile Venus brought a steady rise. On the 11th Sun was square Saturn and the market was so unsteady that there was no quotation. On the 13th Venus par. Mercury brought a rise which was slightly hampered by Sun semi-square Venus on the 15th. On the 17th Venus square brought unexpected anxiety and there was no quotation at all up to 19th. On the 20th

Venus sextile Mercury followed by two good aspects in succession brought a very rapid rise, while Venus semi-square Mercury on the 29th brought an appreciable fall on the next day.

January, 1943.

1. Merc. par. Mars ; Venus opp. Jupiter, 135° Saturn. 2. Merc. par. Jupiter. 3. Venus par. Mars ; Saturn sextile Pluto. 4. Merc. trine Uranus and Neptune. 5. Sun par. Mars ; Venus par. Jupiter. 6. Merc. par. Uranus. 7. Sun 135° Uranus. 8 Merc. trine and par. Saturn, opp. Pluto. 9. Sun par. Jupiter ; Venus trine Uranus. 10. Venus trine Neptune. 11. Sun opp. Jupiter ; Venus semi-sextile Mars. 12. Sun 135° Saturn. 13. Venus trine Saturn, par. Uranus, opp. Pluto. 14. Mars 135° Pluto. 15. Venus par. Saturn. 16. Mercury conj. Venus. 19. Merc. semi-sextile Mars. 20. Sun par. Uranus ; Mars par. Pluto. 21. Sun trine Uranus ; Venus 135° Neptune. 22. Sun trine Neptune ; Merc. opp. Pluto. 23. Sun par. Saturn ; Merc. trine Saturn. 24. Sun conj. Merc. ; Merc. par. Venus. 26. Sun trine Saturn, opp. Pluto. 27. Merc. trine Uranus ; Merc. trine Neptune. 29. Mars square Neptune. 31. Sun par. Merc.

February, 1943.

1. Venus square Uranus. 3. Venus 135° Jupiter. 4. Mars par. Pluto. 5. Venus square Saturn. 6. Sun 135° Neptune. 9. Venus sextile Mars. 10. Mercury semi-square Venus. 14. Venus trine Jupiter. 15. Saturn sextile Pluto. 16. Merc. trine Uranus. 17. Merc. trine Neptune ; Venus 135° Pluto ; Mars 135° Uranus,

opp. Jupiter. 20. Sun 135° Jupiter, square Uranus.
21. Merc. trine Saturn, opp. Pluto ; Mars par. Jupiter.
22. Jupiter semi-square Uranus. 24. Mars 135° Saturn.
25. Sun square Saturn. 26. Venus sextile Uranus, opp.
& par. Neptune. 28. Sun semi-square Mars ; Venus
par. Neptune,

March. 1943.

1. Merc. 135° Neptune ; Venus trine Pluto. 2. Venus sextile Saturn. 6. Sun trine Jupiter. 8. Sun par.
Venus. 9. Venus square Jupiter ; Mars trine Uranus,
trine Neptune. 10. Venus semi-square Uranus. 11. Sun
135° Pluto ; Mercury 135° Jupiter, square Uranus ;
Uranus trine Neptune. 13. Mars par. Uranus. 15. Merc.
square Saturn ; Venus semi-square Saturn ; Mars par.
Saturn, opp. Pluto. 16. Merc. semi-square Venus.
17. Mars trine Saturn. 18. Merc. par. Venus. 19. Sun
par. Neptune. 20. Merc. trine Jupiter. 22. Sun sextile
Uranus, opp. Neptune. 23. Merc. 135° Pluto. 24. Sun
par. Neptune. 26. Sun trine Pluto ; Venus square Pluto.
27. Sun par. Mercury. 28. Merc. semi-square Mars,
opp. Neptune. 29. Sun sextile Saturn ; Merc. sextile
Uranus, par. Neptune ; Mars 135° Neptune. 31. Merc.
par. Neptune, trine Pluto.

April, 1943.

1. Merc. sextile Saturn. 2. Venus par. Mars. 3. Venus 135° Neptune. 4. Sun conj. Merc. ; Venus sextile
Jupiter. 5. Merc. square Jupiter, semi-square Uranus.
6. Sun par. Merc, square Jupiter. 7. Sun semi-square
Uranus. 9. Merc. sextile Mars, semi-square Saturn.
12. Venus par. Saturn. 13. Venus square Mars, par.

Uranus. 14. Merc. par. Mars, square Pluto. 15. Sun semi-square Saturn ; Venus trine Neptune. 17. Venus semi-square Jupiter, conj. Uranus. 19. Merc. 135° Neptune ; Venus sextile Pluto. 20. Venus par. Jupiter ; Mars 135° Jupiter, square Uranus. 21. Sun par. Mars ; Merc. sextile Jupiter ; Jupiter semi-square Uranus. 24. Merc. par. Saturn, par. Uranus ; Venus conj. Saturn; Saturn par. Uranus. 26. Sun square Pluto. 29. Merc. par. Jupiter. 30. Merc. trine Neptune, par. Pluto.

Chart VIII. Jute Market

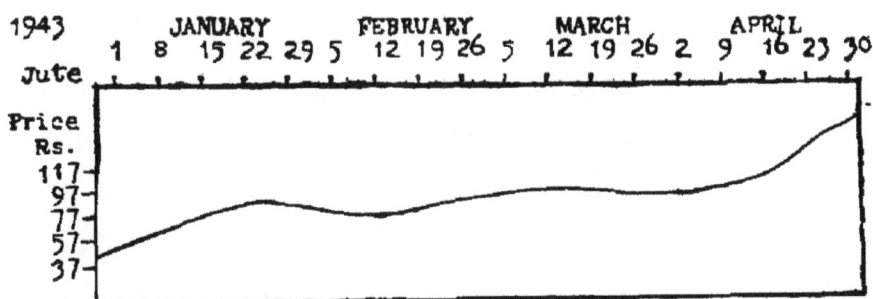

This market is ruled by Venus and Saturn. During January, the majority of the aspects of Venus and Saturn being good, the market rose steadily. In the first week of February the majority of the aspects were evil and the market began to fall up to the middle of the month, after which it rose a little due to Mercury trine Saturn, but no further rise was obtained as the aspects were mixed during the rest of the month. During the first week of March Venus sextile Saturn brought a steady rise, but as the aspects were mixed during the rest of the month, no further rise was obtained, and the price remained about the same level.

In April the majority of the aspects were parallels and benefic, and the market rose steadily throughout the month.

Chart IX. Hessian (B. Twills)

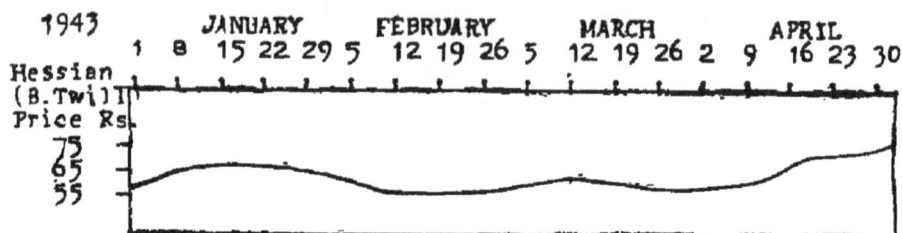

This market is ruled by Venus and Uranus. Due to the majority of good aspects to both the planets the market rose steadily in January. But up to 22nd February the aspects were decidedly evil in majority and the market fell steadily which was stopped by the good aspect Venus sextile Uranus. In March, the majority of the aspects were evil and the market fell gradually but the good aspects to Uranus in the last week checked this fall. The majority of the aspects to these planets in April were parallels after the first week and there were good aspects of Venus, the market rose from the second week in a steady manner.

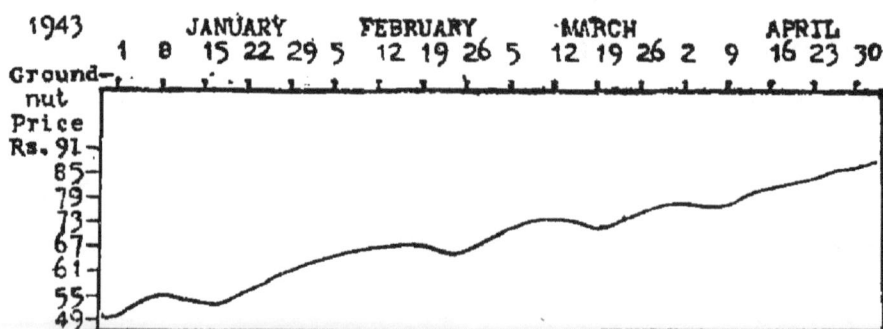

Chart X. Groundnut Market

The seed markets, such as Groundnuts, Linseed, Rapeseed, etc., are ruled by Mercury. During January and February Mercury had plenty of good aspects and the market rose steadily. In March there were evil aspects of Mercury from 11th to 16th and the market fell during this period, but it rose again after the 20th due to the majority of good aspects of Mercury from this date to the end of the month. During April, the majority of good aspects of Mercury kept the market steady and brought a rise.

Bullion Market

The Gold and Silver Markets are now considered for the period of August and September, 1945 as examples.

Chart XI. Gold Market

Price of gold is influenced by the planets transiting the sign Leo or aspecting it according to the good or evil aspects received by them or to the aspects they form with the Sun.

During August, 1945 Mars, Uranus and Neptune were favourably aspecting the sign Leo ; Mercury entered Leo on the 17th. The aspects of the Sun with Jupiter and Neptune and Pluto were evil and the Sun was passing through Leo. Venus was in square aspect with Neptune on the 8th, and Sun was in sextile aspect with Uranus on the 9th. On the 17th Mercury entered Leo being retrograde and was in semi-square aspect with Venus, and Mars was in conjunction with Uranus.

On the 20th the Sun was in conj. with Mercury. On the 26th Mercury was sextile to Mars and on the 24th Mars was parallel to Uranus. The price rose on the 8th to Rs. 78/15, but as there were successive evil aspects up to the 17th the price fell steadily from the 10th up to the 21st to Rs. 64/1. The conjunction of Mercury with the Sun and other good aspects following raised the price to Rs. 71/12.

Uranus, Jupiter, were in favourable aspects to Leo and Mercury and Venus were in Leo in September. Mercury left Leo on the 9th. From the 3rd to 14th we have the following good aspects : 3rd Venus sextile Neptune, 14th Venus sextile Uranus. But on the 10th Sun was in square aspect with Uranus, the price rose slightly to Rs. 73/4. On the 15th Venus was semi-square Jupiter, Mars was square Jupiter and on the 15th the price fell to Rs. 73, and remained down due to Mars square Neptune, on the 17th. On the 18th Jupiter was parallel to Neptune, on the 20th the Sun was parallel to Jupiter and Neptune, 22nd Jupiter conjunction Neptune, 26th Sun parallel Neptune, 27th Mercury parallel Jupiter and Neptune, 28th Sun parallel and conjunction Neptune and on the 30th Mercury conjunction Neptune brought a steady rise in price from the 19th which continued throughout the rest of the month bringing the rise up to Rs. 78.

Chart XII. Silver Market

This market is ruled by the planets Mercury and Saturn and the sign Cancer. The price is affected by the aspects of these planets and also of the planets transiting or aspecting Cancer.

During August Saturn was in Cancer, Neptune in

evil aspect to it, while Jupiter was in good aspect to it up to the 24th and then in evil aspect for the rest of the month. Venus entered Cancer on the 4th and Mercury retrograde was in good aspect with this sign up to the 15th. From the beginning up to the 22nd we have the following aspects : Sun semi-square Jupiter, Mars square Neptune, Mercury semi-square Saturn, Mars parallel Saturn, Mercury semi-square Venus, Venus conjunction Saturn. These show a steady fall and the price fell from Rs. 138 to Rs. 115/8 up to the 24th. On the 26th Mercury was sextile to Mars and the price advanced to 123/12 on the 27th but again fell to Rs. 122/4 on the 28th due to Sun semi-square to Saturn, and again improved by Venus sextile Jupiter on the 31st.

During September, Saturn was in Cancer and Mars entered it on the 8th. Neptune and Jupiter were in aspect with it and Mercury came into aspect with it from the 10th. Up to the 15th we have the good aspects Venus sextile Neptune, Mercury sextile Mars, Sun sextile Saturn and the price rose to Rs. 127/8. After that we have the evil aspects Mercury semi-square Saturn, Venus semi-square Jupiter, Mars and Neptune, Mars square Jupiter and Neptune, and Mercury square Neptune and Uranus up to the 20th and the price came down to Rs. 125/12 on the 15th. From the 22nd we have the good aspects Jupiter conjunction Neptune, Mercury sextile Saturn and conjunction Neptune, and the price steadily rose up to Rs. 135/4 on the 26th.

CHAPTER XXV
Conclusion

In market fluctuations, there are tides almost as regular as those of the Sea. Shakespeare says truly, "There is a tide in affairs of men, which taken at the flood, leads on to fortune."

Some of the tides depend upon the seasons of the year ; business is more active in the spring and summer, and falls off in winter. Supply and Demand being the primary conditions controlling any market, we have only to note that in normal times prices are in inverse proportion to the supply. But this holds good only up to a certain point, for supply cannot of itself create demand. Given peaceful industrial conditions the world over, the world demand of a commodity will very soon be satisfied and any surplus will tend to reduce the market price of the article. War conditions, crop failures and other abnormal conditions, must be dealt with as they arise, and they will inevitably be reflected in the chart of price. These are referred to as artificial factors, and as arising from causes outside of the industry concerned, they have to be sought for from other sources. When a staple article of a country comes under "control" of the Government, it has the immediate effect of suspension of all normal fluctuations. In other respects and in normal times the rules given in this book will be found of great value in buying or selling forward of a commodity.

Besides the influences of the planets, as explained in this book, I consider that the Fixed Stars have also some potent influence in the fluctuations of values as they have influence in other mundane affairs. But this requires further investigation and research before any definite rules can be stated. I believe that they influence in conformity with the general planetary influence as has been already demonstrated, and it would be better if the student keeps a record of their conjunctions and oppositions with the luminaries and the planets and notes whether any serious changes in values of any particular commodity or stock happen during these configurations.

The best guide to Political Predictions and Forecast of war periods, etc., is from Stocks and Shares, these being controlled from political causes rather than from natural sources. For the causes which bring the stocks and share prices to rise and to fall, one might generalize and say that prices in any one market tend to rise when there are good reports of the business activities of the Companies whose shares come within the scope of that market. War means an increase in the demand of money, for considerable sums are required by the Government for the transport and maintenance of troops, the collection of military materials, etc. Also apart from the irrecoverable waste of the means of industrial production in war, external commerce is restricted in consequence of interrupted communications, uncertain markets, but many industrial undertakings would show an increased earning capacity, to

12

be reflected in advancing prices of their stocks and shares. In times of great fluctuations in prices, the investor frequently loses his judgment, particularly when a general feeling of want of commercial confidence occurs. In this book we have shown how the investor can easily determine the cause of the changes of value, and the periodical character of their occurrence and disappearance from the planetary influences, and to enable him to maintain his steadiness of mind, and thus to save his money.

The steller positions accurately indicate the factors in the market, which can "corner" or let the stock out ; can prevent, hinder or suspend the circumstances, rendering the deal profitless, or resulting in a dead loss.

It will be found that the foundation of the rules of planetary influences is sound enough ; proceeding, as it does, upon the principle on which the predictive power of science, which rests upon the uniformity of human motives and actions, is based—that the future will reproduce the past, at least in its main and essential features.

RHYTHM OF LIFE

By F. C. DUTT

NEW, ENLARGED, ENTIRELY REWRITTEN EDITION.

Scientists have demonstrated that all life is rhythmic and there is rhythm in man's "ups and downs" in life. The rhythms work in both sexes, but ordinarily it is difficult to calculate their operation and derive the benefit of knowing about them in advance. In this book for the first time, a simple, scientific method of calculation is clearly explained whereby anyone may *accurately determine* according to biological, cosmical, numerical and psychic rhythms, the fortunate and unfortunate daily, monthly and yearly periods of life ; the state of health, conception of a child of desired sex, or control of birth ; success or failure in an enterprise ; the fate of a nation or country ; the Winner of a Race, Match, Contest ; the price fluctuations of commodities or of Stocks and Shares, Bullions, &c., or anything that is created and brought into existence by natural laws.

These calculations are very easy and require no other helps or any knowledge of Astrology or kindred sciences.

Hitherto all the important events in the World, the events in the life of Netaji Bose, Pundit Nehru, Mahatma Gandhi and his tragic death, and also notable events in the life of many important personages, wars and great events in India and its Independence have been very accurately predicted and demonstrated from the easy rules given in the book and numerous examples have been shown how to apply the rules easily and unerringly.

The rules are extremely simple and easy to apply and will convincingly and very accurately solve all your difficulties in life You will be astonished to find how all your past, present and future events in life can be easily and accurately determined even to the very date by the help of this book ; how you can ascertain the harmony or discord between any two persons ; the disease that afflicts you and the medicine that helps you ; the result of any undertaking ; the actual years of all important events of your life including death : development of psychic power for attainment of power of Fascination, Happiness, Success and Prosperity in life. *You will realize the truth from the very start. Nothing has been exaggerated.*

Secrets never published before are for the first time given out in this book and they are absolutely reliable and will astonish you with their marvellous accuracy ! Every one item is worth many times the price of the book !

Highly spoken of by the Press and Purchasers throughout the World.

"Les conclusions auxquelles il arive sont interessantes et l'ouvrage est d'une lecture agrèable."
—*Sous Le Ciel.* (France.)
"A wonderful book, marvellous and perfectly reliable."
—V. Avelino, Consul of Brazll.

Price Rs. 4/8.   Sh. 7/6. $ 1·50

CHIROLOGICAL SOCIETY

68, AMHERST ROW, Calcutta.

COSMOLOGICAL ECONOMICS

THE MASTERS OF FINANCIAL ASTROLOGY SERIES

The Masters of Financial Astrology Series brings together a collection of the most important classical and modern works on Astroeconomics or astrological financial market forecasting. These classic works written from the Golden Age of Technical Analysis to current times were carefully selected by the late Dr. Jerome Baumring of the Investment Centre Bookstore in the 1980's, as representing the most valuable and important works in financial astrology ever written. They were included as the foundational source texts for his program in advanced financial market analysis and forecasting, and serve as the ideal foundation for any analyst seeking a thorough education in astrological applications to financial market theory and forecasting.

The Golden Age of technical analysis was a period from the early 1900's through the 1960's where the foundational theories of modern financial analysis and financial astrology came into full form. The ideas and technologies developed during this fruitful period include the first serious research into the modern field of Astro-Economics, or Financial Astrology and related fields like cycle analysis, cosmic causation, solar influence on geomagnetic and Earthly events like weather, earthquakes, climate change and radio disturbance. Though financial astrology is actually a subject that stretches back centuries, if not millennia, this ripe period saw the real advent of popular research and theoretical development of this vast study of the interaction between cosmic forces and Earthly phenomena. This collection represents the best work available within this field.

Each quality reprint of these classical texts has been reproduced as an exact facsimile of the original text, maintaining the original layout, typeset, charts, and style of the author and time period, helping to preserve and communicate a sense of the feeling of the original work that a reproduction in modern format does not capture. Many of these rare works and courses were originally printed in only very small private editions or as correspondence courses, so that the originals were easily lost or destroyed over time. Our reproductions of these important source works are printed on acid free paper and bound in a quality hardcover that will compliment any trading library and help to preserve this important resource for generations to come.

The series is also currently being digitized and archived for permanent digital preservation by the Institute of Cosmological Economics, creating a searchable reference library of market wisdom accessible globally and available in new digital formats to keep the knowledge fresh and accessible through new devices and technology as we advance further into the information revolution. To see our full catalog of hardcover reprints, new publications, and digital editions please visit our website at www.CosmoEconomics.com.

- **Professor Weston** - Forecasting The New York Stock Market - *A Treatise on the Geometrical or Chart System of Forecasting* - (1921)
- **Louise McWhirter** - The McWhirter Theory Of Stock Market Forecasting - *The Theory & Application of Forecasting Trends & Cycles* - (1938)
- **James Mars Langham** - Planetary Effects On Stock Market Prices - *The Effects & Applications of Planetary Positions & Aspects on Prices* - (1932)
- **James Mars Langham** - Cyclical Market Forecasting Stocks & Grains - A Complete Course of Instruction in an Original & Proven System - (1938)

❖ **Fakir Chandra Dutt** - Market Forecasting - *A Scientific Exposition Of The Influences Of The Heavenly Bodies On The Fluctuations Of Values* - (1949)

❖ **Richard Scott** - The Planetary Market Barometer - *Trading Stocks, Futures & Forex With Celestial Mechanics* - (2015)

❖ **Fred White, Professor Weston, W. D. Gann, Sepharial** - The Earliest Financial Astrology Manuscripts - *The Original Works of The Old Masters* - (1902)

❖ **Donald Bradley** - Stock Market Prediction - *The Historical & Future Siderograph Charts & Software* - (1948)

❖ **Donald Bradley** - Collected Works of Donald Bradley - *Stock Market Prediction. Picking Winners. The Parallax Problem in Astrology. Solar & Lunar Returns. Profession & Birth Date. Taking the Kid Gloves off Astrology.* - (1950)

❖ **Sepharial (Walter Gorn Old)** - Sepharial's Arcana & Keys - *The Arcana of Stock & Share Key. Key to Sugar Values. Rubber. The Master Key. The Golden Key. The Eclipse System. The Solar Lunar Values. The Solar Apex Method.* - (1930)

❖ **J. Ross Tyler** - Financial Astrology - *The Key To Universal Law* - (1934)

❖ **Dr. Alexander Goulden** - Secrets of the Chronocrators - *An Advanced Course in Astrological Forecasting of Financial Markets* - (2014)

❖ **Dr. Alexander Goulden** - Behind the Veil - *Celestial Mechanics & Ancient Geometry in Financial Analysis* - (2010)

❖ **Daniele Prandelli** - The Law Of Cause And Effect - *Creating A Planetary Price/Time Map Of Market Action Through Sympathetic Resonance* - (2010)

❖ **T. G. Butaney, Financial Astrologer** - Forecasting Prices - *A Complete Course of Commercial Astrology* - (1940)

❖ **T. G. Butaney, Financial Astrologer** - How To Forecast Prices & Winners In Horse Races - *With Astrological Forecast Of Prices Or Cotton, Grains, Oil-Seeds & Rainfall* - (1947)

❖ **T. G. Butaney, Financial Astrologer** - Master Key Of Races - *All My Numerological & Astrological Secrets Discovered Over 30 Years' Experience* - (1970)

❖ **William D. Gann** - Collected Writings of W. D. Gann, Volume III - *Master Mathematical Formula, Calculators & Astrological Writings* - (1955)

- ❖ **Muriel & Louis Hasbrouck** – Space Time Forecasting of Economic Trends – (1958-1006)

- ❖ **George Bayer** - Money Investing In Stocks, Trading In Commodities, Or The Time Factors In The Stock Market - *The Art of Scientifically Detecting Direction & Distance of Swings* - (1937)

- ❖ **George Bayer** - A Complete Course In Astrology - *Erection & Interpretation Of Horoscopes As Well As For Stocks* - (1937)

- ❖ **George Bayer** - Turning Four Hundred Years Of Astrology To Practical Use & Other Matters - (1944)

- ❖ **George Bayer** - Bible Interpretation - (1937)

- ❖ **Daniel T. Ferrera** - Studies In Astrological Bible Interpretation - (2001)

- ❖ **George J. McCormack** - Long-Range Astro-Weather Forecasting - *A Private, Comprehensive Technical Instruction Course* - (1965)

- ❖ **George J. McCormack** - ASTROTECH – *A Collection of Journals on Astrological Finance* - (1937-1941)

- ❖ **John Nelson** - Cosmic Patterns - (2006)

- ❖ **Thomas H. Graydon** - New Laws For Natural Phenomena - (1938)

- ❖ **W. T. Foster** - Sun Spots And Weather - (1907)

- ❖ **Cornelius Walford** - Famines Of The World - *Past & Present* - (1879)

- ❖ **Prof. Jos. Rodes Buchanan, M. D.** - Periodicity - *The Law Of All Life* - (1912)

- ❖ **Ray & Josephine Smythe** - Stars Ahead - (1942)

- ❖ **Sam Bartolet** - Eclipses & Lunations In Astrology - (1937)

- ❖ **Effie M. Cooley** - Astrological Relation Of Names & Numbers - (1912)

- ❖ **L. Edward Johndro** - Collected L. Edward Johndro - *The Stars, How And Where They Influence. The Earth in the Heavens. A New Concept of Sign Rulership. Astrological Dictionary & Self-Reading Horoscope* - (1927)

- ❖ **L. Edward Johndro** - Johndro's Collected Articles - 1930's - (1930)

- ❖ **Maurice Wemyss** - The Wheel Of Life Or Scientific Astrology - *5 Volumes Bound in 2 Hardcovers* - (1927)

- ❖ **Robert DeLuce** - Rectification Of The Horoscope - *Practical Lessons, Tables & Illustrations* - (1930)

- ❖ **Fred White** - A Guide To Astrology - *& Correcting The Time Of Birth* - (1901)

- ❖ **Gregorius** - The Master Key Of Destiny - (1924)
- ❖ **Paul Councel** - Your Stars And Destiny - (1940)
- ❖ **Mark Mellen** - How To Play The Races And Win - (1938)